GREG LAURIE

DO YOU WANT TO

CHANGE

Your Life?

GREG LAURIE

DO YOU WANT TO
CHANGE
Your Life?

ALLEN
DAVID
BOOKS

Art direction: Greg Laurie
Art production: Mark Ferjulian
Cover design: Michael Berger

ISBN 978-1-942090-08-3

Cataloging-in-Publication Data is available.
Printed in India

1 2 3 4 5 6 7 8 / 20 19 18 17 16 15

CONTENTS

INTRODUCTION

In every Harvest Crusade, wherever we may be in the world, I always close each event the same way.

The settings for these crusades might vary a great deal. Being in Dallas doesn't feel much like being in Philadelphia, and New York City doesn't resemble Anaheim, Australia, or New Zealand. We may be inside some great hall or sports arena, or outside in a large stadium. It may be in daylight or at night under the lights. The music will vary, as different bands, artists, and singers share the platform. A variety of guest speakers will talk about their walk with Christ or how they came to know the Lord. And of course I have preached scores of different messages through the years.

Wherever we are, however, the need never changes.

People need to know Jesus, and at the close of each crusade, no matter where we may be, I give them a chance to make a decision to follow Jesus Christ. There is a clear method in what I share in a crusade message, but it's really no different than what I would say if I were talking to someone about Christ one-on-one. It's a method you can use when you share your faith. It's simple, it's Bible-centered, and people of all ages from all over the world can easily understand it.

Everyone on our team knows pretty much what I will say in those closing moments of a crusade, and they are praying with me as I say it. At the end of each message I make five final points. The precise wording might not be the same, but the main ideas are there every time. On any given night at a Harvest Crusade, it might sound something like this. . . .

#1: YOU NEED TO ADMIT YOU ARE A SINNER

This is difficult for some. People choke on that word. *Me? A sinner?* Yes, you, and yes, all of us. The Bible says, "For all have sinned and fall short of the glory of God" (Romans 3:23). To sin means to cross a line, and we have all done that. We have all stepped over the line. We have all broken the commandments.

Someone will say, "Okay, I've broken a few of them. But I'm not as bad as some people." That may be true. Unfortunately, God doesn't grade on the curve. Even *one* sin is enough to keep you out of Heaven. The Bible says, "Whoever shall keep the whole law, and yet stumble in one point, he is guilty of all" (James 2:10).

Here's the bottom line: You have to come clean and admit it. You, I, us—we are all sinners.

#2: YOU NEED TO RECOGNIZE THAT JESUS CHRIST DIED ON THE CROSS FOR YOUR SIN

Jesus said, "Greater love has no one than this, than to lay down one's life for his friends" (John 15:13). Two thousand years ago, Jesus allowed Himself to be crucified on a Roman cross, and bled and died for us. He wasn't taken against His will. He went willingly. Why did He walk that path? Why did He do that? Because He loves us, and it was our only hope to escape Hell and gain Heaven.

#3: YOU NEED TO REPENT OF YOUR SIN

To repent means to change your mind, to change your direction. The Bible says, "God . . . now commands all men everywhere to repent" (Acts 17:30). But here's the problem. There are many people today who think they are Christians, but who have never repented. They have never changed the direction of their lives. They say that they love God, but they continually break His commandments and live in opposition to His Word. And that just won't work. If you truly love God you will do what He says. If you love God you will keep His commandments. When you repent, that means you turn from your sin, and start on a new direction in life.

#4: YOU NEED TO RECEIVE CHRIST INTO YOUR LIFE

The Bible says, "But as many as received Him, to them He gave the right to become children of God, to those who believe in His name" (John 1:12). Jesus says, "Behold, I stand at the door and knock. If anyone hears My voice and opens the door, I will come in to him and dine with him, and he with Me" (Revelation 3:20). Only you can open the door of your heart. Jesus won't kick it down. He won't pick the lock or force His way into your life. You must receive Him as Savior and Lord.

It's like receiving a gift from a friend. Imagine that someone hands you a nicely wrapped present, and says, "Here. I bought this for you. Take it." Will you open your hands and receive the present, or will you turn away from your friend and reject that gift? For a gift to be a gift, it has to be received. And that's the way it is with God. He offers us the forgiveness of our sins and eternal life in Heaven as a gift. Will you accept it or reject it? It's a choice every one of us must make for ourselves.

#5: YOU NEED TO DO IT PUBLICLY

This is something I say when I am standing in front of a stadium full of people, inviting them to receive Christ as Savior. If they have made a commitment to Jesus, I ask them to stand to their feet and walk to the front of the stadium or hall or wherever we are meeting.

Why do I ask people to make a public commitment? Because Jesus says, "Everyone who acknowledges me publicly here on earth, I will also acknowledge before my Father in heaven. But everyone who denies me here on earth, I will also deny before my Father in heaven" (Matthew 10:32-33, NLT).

By making your decision to follow Jesus publicly, you are saying, in effect, "I don't care who sees. I don't care who knows. I know that what I have heard tonight is true, and I'm ready to make a stand. I'm not going to keep my faith a secret. I'm going to speak about it to others."

You may not be in a public meeting when you receive Jesus Christ, but you can make it public by sharing your decision with others and telling them what your new life in the Lord means to you.

#6: YOU NEED TO DO IT NOW

Don't say, *"I'll just put all this on the back burner and think about it later. . . . I'll be sure to respond at the NEXT Harvest Crusade. . . . I'll do this tomorrow morning after I sleep on it."* The Bible says, "Now is the accepted time; behold, now is the day of salvation" (2 Corinthians 6:2).

Now is the time, and *today* is the day. None of us know for sure that we will still be alive on the planet tomorrow morning—or even an hour from now. Don't miss your appointment! This is your moment. This is your opportunity.

The Task Belongs to All of Us

It's true that not all of us are called to be full-time evangelists. There are men and women who are uniquely gifted as evangelists, like Billy Graham, Franklin Graham, Luis Palau, and others.

No, we're not all called to be evangelists, but we are all called to *evangelize*. Every one of us has the same set of marching orders from the Lord Himself. Just before He left the Earth for Heaven, He said these words:

"All authority has been given to Me in heaven and on earth. Go therefore and make disciples of all the nations, baptizing them in the name of the Father and of the Son and of the Holy Spirit, teaching them to observe all things that I have commanded you; and lo, I am with you always, even to the end of the age" (Matthew 28:18-20).

In the original language, the clear implication is that these words are addressed to everyone who knows the Lord. This isn't just for pastors or missionaries or full-time evangelists. No, this command is for business people, homemakers, students, doctors, plumbers, football players, ballet dancers, and accountants. In other words, it is for all who know Him. Jesus isn't saying, "I would really appreciate this if you can work it into your busy schedule. I know you have so much going on, but as a personal favor to Me would you mind going into all the world and preaching the gospel?"

No, our Commander in Chief actually orders us to do so.

The book you hold in your hands will help you follow that command. As you read through my crusade messages, my prayer is that it will stir up your heart to do the same on a personal level.

The important thing is not that you are preaching to thousands in stadiums or millions on TV and radio. The important thing is obeying your Lord and making the most of every opportunity where you are right now.

Greg Laurie
Riverside, California
2015

1

GOD'S CURE FOR HEART TROUBLE

Have you ever been stressed out to the max?

You know what I'm talking about. It was one of those days when everything seemed to go wrong. And then, just when you thought it couldn't get any worse, it got worse.

We've had television, radio, and newspapers for years that have brought us scary news with our morning coffee. But now those dark and frightening news stories go with us absolutely everywhere on our smartphones, tablets, and laptops—and now, even on our watches! Of course, every night of the week on television, cable news recycles all those stories in an endless loop.

Other people in earlier generations might have believed they lived in an information age, but we *really* do. Virtually everyone has a cell phone now. I read recently that 42 percent of Americans say they simply can't live without their cell phones. Half of Americans sleep with their cell phones next to their beds.[1]

I remember when the first mobile phone came out. It was a car model. If you were in your car, you could talk on your phone. But then they came out with the first truly mobile model, made by Motorola. It was the size of a World

War II walkie-talkie and had a battery life of about nine minutes.

I can actually remember seeing my very first mobile phone. A friend of mine met me for lunch, and he pulled the thing out of his briefcase. I said, "What is that? Is that a *mobile phone*? That is so cool!" Hardly anyone had them back then.

Now everyone has them. They practically give them to babies at birth. *Here is your mobile phone, sweetie. Push this button for a picture of Mommy—and this one when you need your diaper changed.* They even have bone-shaped cell phones for dogs. I'm not kidding. It hangs around the dog's neck so you can talk to him or call him if he runs off somewhere. Poor dog. It probably traumatizes him. He's running around and then suddenly hears in his ear, "Come home!" (By the way, they don't make cell phones for cats. Cats wouldn't even respond. You could call the cat all day long, and he would say to himself, "Right. As if I'm going to answer that!")

One effect of all this information flooding the airwaves is more and more stress for everyone. You seemingly can't get away from it. As a result, our nation today has more depression and nervous breakdowns. Some medical experts say they've even found links between stress and diseases like cancer. The Centers for Disease Control and Prevention estimate that up to 90 percent of visits to doctors in the United States are triggered by a stress-related illness.[2]

That's why so many people are taking prescription drugs now. There were 46 million prescriptions for Xanax, an antianxiety drug, given out in 2010.[3] Women are twice as likely to feel anxious and frightened as men, and young people are more likely to feel afraid than older people. (I guess that means if you're a young woman, you're pretty stressed out much of the time.)

In the United Kingdom they have actually installed cameras on practically every street corner, just to make people feel safer. As a result, however, many Brits are nervous about the cameras and feel more paranoid than ever. So what do you do?

I heard a story about a man who was very ill and asked his wife to go with him to see the doctor. So the doctor met with the man for a while, ran some tests, and then asked to speak privately with the man's wife.

"I want to talk to you about your husband," the doctor said. "He is very ill and could die soon. He has a disease that is triggered by stress. So here is what you need to do. You need to create a stress-free environment for him. By that I mean don't give him any jobs to do—no chores . . . smother him with affection . . . tell him how much you love him. Make him his favorite meal for breakfast . . . a gourmet meal for lunch . . . something wonderful for dinner. Create this wonderful, stress-free life for six months to a year, and he will make a full recovery."

The woman thanked the doctor, left the office, and joined her husband in the car.

"What did the doctor say?" her husband asked.

She looked at him and said, "You're going to die."

Seriously though, we live in a frightening world. Rogue

states like North Korea—and now Iran—have developed nuclear weapons technology. Terrorist groups like ISIS behead people on video. The threat of terrorism casts a shadow over every corner of the globe.

Then we have random acts of violence. A man walks into a movie theater and starts shooting total strangers. Another walks into a school and opens fire. Another begins a shooting spree in a church.

So Many Fears

Time magazine did a cover story on the topic of fear, listing what people in our nation are afraid of these days. The author pointed out that fifty million people in the United States have some kind of fear or phobia.[4]

I can understand some of those fears—like the fear of flying, a fear of heights, or the fear of small places. But then there are some phobias I'd never heard of before. There is ablutophobia, the fear of washing or bathing; dentophobia, the fear of dentists; and cyclophobia, the fear of bicycles.

And then, in my estimation, these fears get downright strange. There is alektorophobia, the fear of chickens (apparently you break out in a cold sweat when you drive by a KFC or a Chick-fil-A); allodoxaphobia, the fear of other people's opinions; lutraphobia, the fear of otters (Otters? Seriously?); ecclesiophobia, the fear of church; hadephobia, the fear of Hell; and ouranophobia, the fear of Heaven.

There is also peladophobia, the fear of baldness or bald people. I hope you don't have that fear, because that would make me your worst nightmare, especially if you also have ecclesiophobia, hadephobia, and ouranophobia and come hear me preach at church on the afterlife.

The simple truth is that life is filled with things that cause fear, and I believe there are more troubled, anxious people in our nation than ever before. In the message that follows, I want to share with you what Jesus had to say to people with troubled hearts.

You might call it a cure for heart trouble.

What Jesus Says about Peace

I read an article recently about Simon Cowell, a British multimillionaire producer and entertainer with television programs like *American Idol* and *The X Factor* to his credit.

According to the article, however, Cowell recently had a breakdown. He was bedridden for a week, cutting himself off from everyone. He confided to a friend, "I don't want any more tablets and pills. I'm cutting out the lot, including cigarettes. I desperately need peace. I'm craving normality. I've got to work out my demons and come out of it. . . . I have to stop reading texts at 3:00 a.m. and making calls later and later."

He concluded, "I want peace."[5]

Yes, Simon, you do. We all do. We need the peace that only God can provide.

In John 14:1–6, Jesus made some simple declarations that have shone like a light in our troubled world for over two thousand years:

"Let not your heart be troubled; you believe in

God, believe also in Me. In My Father's house are many mansions; if it were not so, I would have told you. I go to prepare a place for you. And if I go and prepare a place for you, I will come again and receive you to Myself; that where I am, there you may be also. And where I go you know, and the way you know."

Thomas said to Him, "Lord, we do not know where You are going, and how can we know the way?"

Jesus said to him, "I am the way, the truth, and the life. No one comes to the Father except through Me."

Just before He spoke these comforting words, Jesus had dropped a bombshell on His men, revealing that He would soon be arrested, beaten, and crucified.

For most of us who have heard at least part of the story of Jesus, there's no longer any shock value in those words. But for these men who had followed Jesus for several years, it was like the end of everything. They didn't yet understand that Jesus was going to the cross to die for the sins of the world and be raised again after three days.

All they heard was that He was about to leave them.

And Jesus was saying, "Listen, men . . . don't let your hearts be troubled."

The word *troubled* could be translated "agitated," "disturbed," or "thrown into confusion." Another translation puts it this way: "Don't let your heart shudder."

In modern vernacular, He was saying, "Don't panic."

The disciples were probably thinking, *Don't panic?? Are you kidding me? How can we not panic when He's talking about leaving us . . . being arrested by the Romans . . . dying on a cross?*

Jesus then gave them three reasons they shouldn't be afraid and shouldn't have a troubled heart.

REASON 1: WE CAN TAKE GOD AT HIS WORD

If you want to get rid of your heart trouble, your stress, and your fear, you have to take God at His word. Jesus said in John 14: "Believe also in Me." In Greek it has the force of a command: *"Believe in Me."*

Do you believe in God? I'm not speaking here about simply believing there is a God. Most Americans believe that. But do you know God in a personal way?

Actor George Clooney once stated, "I don't believe in heaven and hell. I don't know if I believe in God. All I know is that as an individual, I won't allow this life—the only thing I know to exist—to be wasted."[6]

Robert De Niro said, "If heaven exists, I would say to God, 'You've got a lot of explaining to do.' "[7]

Really? I think it might be someone else who needs to do the explaining.

Actor Kevin Costner is more helpful and hopeful on the topic. He said in an interview, "I have always wanted to believe that there is something more to life than what we have here on earth."

He was then asked, "Do you believe in heaven?"

Costner replied, "I desperately want to! I mean, I really want to believe that a part of me will continue on after this life and that there's more to me and to this life than just what's here on Earth. Yes, I want to believe."[8]

Jesus says to him and to everyone else, "Believe in Me."

Yes, Jesus was about to die on a cross, but the result would be eternal salvation for millions and millions of people.

We all face tragedy in life. When deep disappointments or major crises hit our lives, people around us may offer words of "comfort" that really aren't very comforting.

Someone will say, "Hey, it's all good, man."

No, it isn't.

"When life gives you lemons, make lemonade."

"When the going gets tough, the tough get going."

"What doesn't kill you only makes you stronger."

Those are all lame, really useless clichés. I have a better one, right from the pages of the Bible: "And we know that all things work together for good to those who love God, to those who are the called according to His purpose" (Romans 8:28).

Now *that* is comfort. Do you know what that means? It means that even when tragedy strikes, God can bring good despite the bad. It doesn't mean that good *becomes* bad. No, bad is bad, a crisis is a crisis, and a tragedy is a tragedy.

But notice that Romans 8:28 says, "All things work together for good *to those who love God*" (emphasis added). You have to love God before all of your heartache, tragedy, and anxieties work together for good in your life.

Do you love God? I can tell you with no hesitation that God loves you! He loves you no matter who you are, where you've been, or what you have done.

In John 14 Jesus is saying, "Believe in God. Trust that I know what I'm doing, even if you don't understand it all right now."

Take God at His word. Looking back at my life since I became a Christian, I have found that the Word of God has sustained me through the most difficult, heartbreaking days of my life. I can truly say with the psalmist, "You are my refuge and my shield; I have put my hope in your word" (Psalm 119:114, NIV).

If you are a Christian, you have hope—even in the face of death. You have hope that you will be reunited with your believing loved ones one day in Heaven and on the new Earth. You will see them again. They won't only be a part of your past, but they will be a part of your future— forever.

Sometimes believers speak of the afterlife. And yes, there is an afterlife. At the same time, however, we might very well call these days on Earth the "beforelife." This is the small part of life; the big part is later. This life is like watching a short trailer of a movie. It's just a foretaste, or preview, of what's to come.

You are the one who must decide (perhaps this very day) where you will spend your eternity.

The options are Heaven and Hell.

That's it. There are no other options.

Just as surely as there is a God in Heaven who loves you, there is a Hell. But God didn't make Hell for people. Jesus said that Hell was created for the Devil and his angels (see Matthew 25:41). God has done everything He can to keep you out of Hell, sending His own Son Jesus to Earth to die on the cross in your place and pay the price and penalty for your sin. If you will turn from that sin and trust in Jesus, you can go to Heaven when you die.

You can know it for sure. You need never wonder again.

REASON 2: IF YOU ARE A CHRISTIAN, YOU WILL GO TO HEAVEN

Jesus said, "In My Father's house are many mansions; if it were not so, I would have told you. I go to prepare a place for you" (John 14:2).

Heaven is real. It's as real of a place as Los Angeles, New York, or Chicago. Maybe you love the city where you live. Maybe you have some good beaches and great restaurants and cultural attractions. But it also has problems, just like every city on Earth. Heaven will be all the greatest things we love about cities, but without the bad and sad parts. And we will be able to enjoy it for all eternity.

Heaven is not a state of mind. Heaven is not some wispy, misty, ethereal realm in the clouds. It is an actual place that we will go to if we trust in Christ.

The late science fiction writer Isaac Asimov wrote, "I don't believe in an afterlife, so I don't have to spend my whole life fearing hell, or fearing heaven even more. For whatever the tortures of hell, I think the boredom of heaven would even be worse."[9]

What an absurd comment. Asimov might have been a brilliant writer, but on this issue he didn't know what he was talking about. Heaven will be a place of activity, a place of service to the King, and a place of reuniting with loved ones who have gone on before us.

I love the description that the writer to the Hebrews gives us:

> You have come right up into Mount Zion, to the city of the living God, the heavenly Jerusalem, and to the gathering of countless happy angels; and to the church, composed of all those registered in heaven; and to God who is Judge of all; and to the spirits of the redeemed in heaven, already made perfect; and to Jesus himself, who has brought us his wonderful new agreement.
> (Hebrews 12:22–24, TLB)

C. S. Lewis said, "Heaven is not a state a mind. Heaven is reality itself."[10] He also said, "All the things that have ever deeply possessed your soul have been but hints of [Heaven]—tantalizing glimpses, promises never quite fulfilled, echoes that died away just as they caught your ear."[11]

That is why nothing this world offers will satisfy you: no drug, no degree hanging on your wall, no amount of money, no car, no high-tech toys, no sexual experience, no man, no woman, no stellar career. Deep inside, each of us longs for Heaven and a relationship with the living God.

It's like a great, gaping hole in our hearts that we try to fill with everything else, but nothing really fills up that space except God Himself.

An interviewer from *Rolling Stone* recently asked the actor Charlie Sheen, "What's that empty spot inside that you're trying to fill?"

"Not sure," Sheen responded. "I don't know what that is."

The interviewer persisted, "Do you ever feel like you are searching for something?"

Charlie Sheen responded, "Yeah, sure. . . . Don't know for what, though. But I do feel like I'm going to meet some wizard guide someday who will sort of lay it out for me."[12]

But Charlie Sheen doesn't need a wizard guide. He needs to open up the Bible—the ultimate user's manual of life—and listen to the words of Jesus. He will tell him what he is looking for.

Knowing that Heaven awaits us in our near future helps us deal with the hardships and disappointments and challenges in this life. No matter what the pain or struggle, it is nothing compared to the great hope that awaits us just around the corner.

In his letter to the church at Corinth, Paul wrote,

> For our present troubles are small and won't last very long. Yet they produce for us a glory that vastly outweighs them and will last forever! So we don't look at the troubles we can see now; rather, we fix our gaze on things that cannot be

seen. For the things we see now will soon be gone,
but the things we cannot see will last forever.
(2 Corinthians 4:17–18, NLT)

Why should I not have a troubled heart? First, believe God and that His Word, the Bible, is true.

Second, remember that if you are a Christian, you will go to Heaven.

And here is a third reason.

REASON 3: JESUS CHRIST IS COMING BACK AGAIN

Jesus said He would come again. And I personally believe that His coming could be very soon.

If I walked outside with you and noticed that the sky was dark with rain clouds, and a cool wind began to blow, what would you think if I prophesied that it was going to rain?

You might reply, "Well, you're really not much of a prophet. It's obvious that it's going to rain."

By the way, bald men are always the first to know when it's raining. Not long ago I was walking with my wife, who has a lot of hair. It's very thick. What she casts off her brush every day would be like a revival on my head.

As we were walking, I said, "Cathe, it's starting to rain."

"No, it's not," she said.

"Trust me," I said, "it's raining. Bald men always know first. You might not be ready to make that call for probably ten minutes."

And sure enough, eventually she felt the rain too.

Most of us are aware that it's about to rain because we see the signs in the sky. And the same thing is true about the return of Jesus Christ. We know that event is drawing near because we see the signs of the times all around us. We see and read about specific situations and events in our world today, and we know these are the very things the Bible tells us will happen in the last days before Christ's return.

It's on the front pages of the newspapers.

It's on television news.

It's on the Internet and our favorite websites—reminders that the day of Jesus' return to Earth is nearer than ever. Again, Jesus said in John 14, "I will come again and receive you to Myself; that where I am, there you may be also" (verse 3).

Notice our Lord's word choice here. He didn't say, "I will take you." Rather, He said, "I will *receive* you." In other words, He won't take you against your will. If you don't want to be with Jesus, you don't have to. If you don't want to spend your eternity in Heaven, God doesn't require you to. He is coming to *receive* those who are waiting for Him and looking for Him. Hebrews 9:28 says that "to those who eagerly wait for Him He will appear a second time."

The New Testament tells us that when Jesus comes for His church, it will be "in a flash, in the twinkling of an eye" (1 Corinthians 15:52, NIV). The Bible says that "the Lord Himself will descend from heaven with a shout, with the voice of an archangel, and with the trumpet of God. And the dead in Christ will rise first. Then we who are alive and remain shall be caught up together with them in the clouds to meet the Lord in the air. And thus we shall always be with the Lord" (1 Thessalonians 4:16–17).

When Jesus comes for us, there will be a great family reunion "in the clouds." We will be reunited with Christian loved ones and with the Lord Himself.

Maybe you would say, "I'm not so sure about that, Greg. Some of my family members are pretty weird. I have this strange uncle."

But in Heaven, all of the weirdness and strangeness will be gone. It will be a glorious family reunion. We will sing together, reminisce together, and even eat together. Yes, we *are* going to eat in the next life. Isn't that good news?

Once again, when it happens, it will happen in a heartbeat. Jesus said that two will be working together in a field when one will be taken and the other left. Two will be lying in bed, and one will be taken and the other left.

A number of years ago, I was lying in bed with my wife late at night, and she was saying to me, "Greg, isn't it wonderful that one night we might just fall asleep and wake up in Heaven?"

Admittedly, I'm a bit of a prankster. While she was still talking about this, I slipped out of bed and got down on the floor.

She said, "Wouldn't that be great, Greg? . . . Greg? . . . GREG? GREG!!"

It will happen like that, but it won't be a joke. Millions of people will be caught up in the air to meet the Lord, but millions more will be left behind.

If Jesus came tonight, would you be ready?

You Have a Choice

The fact is that you have a choice before you. You can get right, or you can *get left*. I'm not talking politics here. I'm speaking about getting right with God. If you aren't right with God when Christ returns for His church, then you will be left behind.

Maybe you would say, "I don't know, Greg. I'm still a little skeptical."

I have some good news for you: Jesus loves skeptics.

In John 14, the chapter we've been considering, we pick up on a conversation between Jesus and Thomas. Jesus had been saying,

> "And if I go and prepare a place for you, I will come again and receive you to Myself; that where I am, there you may be also. And where I go you know, and the way you know."
>
> Thomas said to Him, "Lord, we do not know where You are going, and how can we know the way?"
>
> Jesus said to him, "I am the way, the truth, and the life. No one comes to the Father except through Me." (verses 3–6)

I love Thomas because he was so honest. Thomas was the kind of guy who thought for himself. Sometimes he is called Doubting Thomas, but I think of him more as *Skeptical* Thomas. He didn't let others do his thinking for him.

I, too, was a skeptic about Christ for many years. I thought to myself, *This Christianity thing won't work for me. I'm not the religious type. Christ could never change a person like me.*

But He did.

Jesus is an expert at changing skeptics into believers. In fact, it has been said that skepticism is the first step to belief.

Jesus had another encounter with Thomas after He rose from the dead. He had appeared to the disciples in a room, but Thomas wasn't there when He appeared. When they saw Thomas, they were understandably excited.

"Hey, Thomas! Guess who showed up last night? *Jesus!*"

"Yeah, right."

"No, really!"

"Well, I won't believe it until I can put my hand in the wound in His side and touch the wounds in His hands."

The next time they all got together, Thomas included, Jesus showed up again:

> And after eight days His disciples were again inside, and Thomas with them. Jesus came, the doors being shut, and stood in the midst, and said, "Peace to you!" Then He said to Thomas, "Reach your finger here, and look at My hands; and reach your hand here, and put it into My side. Do not be unbelieving, but believing."
>
> And Thomas answered and said to Him, "My Lord and my God!"
>
> (John 20:26–28)

Earlier Thomas had asked his question, "Lord, we do not know where You are going, and how can we know the way?" (John 14:5). And we can be glad about that question, because it led to one of the greatest answers in all the Bible. Jesus said, "I am the way, the truth, and the life. No one comes to the Father except through Me" (verse 6).

In today's culture, that statement is highly controversial. People today like to believe in diversity and in many roads to Heaven. They don't like to hear that Jesus is the only way to God. In fact, most Americans don't agree that He is.

A Barna poll revealed that half of all Americans believe that if a person is generally good or does enough good things for others during his or her lifetime, that individual will earn a place in Heaven.

But that is not what the Bible teaches.

Besides that, what is your definition of *good*? I have noticed that the definition varies from person to person. What one person says is good, another may say is bad. Most of us don't even live up to our own standards of what we regard as good.

Are there good people out there?

Certainly.

Are there good people who aren't Christians?

Yes, there are.

It's not about whether you are a good person. The point here is that you are not good enough because you are not perfect. No one is except God Himself.

You, in fact, are a sinner, just like I am. That's where Jesus comes in. Jesus is the Savior. And He will be your Savior if you will ask for His forgiveness.

The Good News

Some people may be worse than others, but none of us are as good as we think. We are all sinners, according to the Scriptures, and even one sin would be enough to keep us out of Heaven.

You could take all of the other religions of the world and sum them up in one word: do. Do this, and maybe you will go to Heaven. Do this, and you will reach nirvana or achieve some elevated state of mind.

But in contrast to the religions of the world that say *do*, Jesus Christ says, "*Done*. I paid for it at the cross. It is finished. You can be forgiven."

"Yes," some will protest, "but how can you say that Jesus is the *only* way?"

I *didn't* say it. Jesus did.

Jesus is the only one who ever lived who was qualified to bridge the gap between humanity and God. Why? Because Jesus wasn't just a good man; Jesus was the God-man. He was God in human form, walking among us. So when He voluntarily went to the cross and died for our sin, here is what He did: With one hand He took hold of a holy God, and with the other hand He took hold of sinful humanity. He bridged the gap between God and man. The book of Colossians says it like this: "God made you alive with Christ, for he forgave all our sins. He canceled the record of the charges against us and took it away by nailing it to the cross" (2:13–14, NLT).

The Bible says, "Salvation is found in no one else, for there is no other name under heaven given to mankind by which we must be saved" (Acts 4:12, NIV).

I read an interview where Paul McCartney talked about his views on God. Here is what Sir Paul said: "I believe in a spirit. That's the best I can put it. I think there is something greater than us, and I love it, and I am grateful to it, but just like everyone else on the planet, I can't pin it down. I'm happy not pinning it down. I pick bits out of all the religions—so I like many things that Buddhists say, I like a lot of things that Jesus said, that Mohammed said."

Then he concludes, "Be cool and you'll be all right. That's rock & roll religion."[13]

"Be cool and you'll be all right?"

That may be rock-and-roll religion, but it isn't true. No, I think it is time for him to "let it be" and go to the only expert. Jesus said, "I am the way, the truth, and the life. No one comes to the Father except through Me."

"But that's so narrow-minded!" some would say. "I believe that as long as people are sincere in their beliefs, they can follow any path they want, and it will get them to Heaven."

Come on. Do you really believe that?

Imagine yourself inside of a 737 on the runway, preparing to fly to Hawaii. Your tray table is in the upright and locked position, you're buckled in, and you're ready to begin your journey. Then you hear the voice of the captain over the intercom.

"Good morning, ladies and gentlemen. Welcome to flight 242, with direct service to Honolulu, Hawaii. Our cruising altitude will be 32,000 feet. We will be showing a movie."

This is all sounding good, and you're beginning to relax a little. And then the pilot says this: "By the way, folks. I'm not so sure about this whole *fuel thing*. The gauge in front of me is indicating that we don't have enough fuel to reach Hawaii. But I think we will make it! Don't worry, because I feel really good about this.

"In fact, I feel so good about it that I'm going to turn off our navigation equipment, turn off the map, and fly by dead reckoning. All of those maps and charts are too narrow-minded! You see, folks, I believe that all roads lead to Hawaii. There's no need for anyone to worry, because I am very sincere about all of this. So sit back, relax, and enjoy the flight."

What would you think in such a moment? You would be yelling, "Get me off this plane! There's a psycho in the cockpit!"

We might laugh at an imaginary scenario like that, but it has strong parallels to reality. The most important journey that you and I ever will take is the one into eternity. There will be no turning back from that journey! It's forever.

To gamble with your eternity is a much more serious matter than gambling with a flight to Hawaii. Jesus said,

"You can enter God's Kingdom only through the narrow gate. The highway to hell is broad, and its gate is wide for the many who choose that way. But the gateway to life is very narrow and the road is difficult, and only a few ever find it" (Matthew 7:13–14, NLT).

We need to follow our Captain! Hebrews 2:10 calls Jesus "the captain of [our] salvation."

When I fly out of LAX, I can't just walk through security and board any plane I want to. No, I must have proper identification to walk to my gate and board the plane.

God offers you a ticket to Heaven itself. It was bought for you at the cross of Calvary. But you have to *receive* that ticket.

You do that by admitting you are a sinner, turning from your sin, and believing in Jesus as your Savior and Lord.

Without a doubt, it is the most important decision that you ever will make.

2 Chapter

HOME

BEFORE DARK

From the moment you were born, you have been on a quest.

What you have been after perhaps hasn't been completely clear, but through the years you have wanted your life to have some kind of purpose and meaning. You have wanted to know why you are here on this earth.

And you wanted to be happy.

It has been said that two things are true of every person: we all want to be happy, and we are all going to die.

From the very earliest moments of our lives, we are on this search, this quest. A philosopher named Hugh Moorhead once wrote to 250 of the best-known philosophers, scientists, writers, and intellectuals around the country. He asked them a simple question: "In your opinion what is the meaning of life?"

Some offered their best guesses. Some admitted that they simply made up a purpose for life. Many wrote Moorhead, asking if *he* had discovered the meaning of life.

What was true of those intellectuals and experts is true of most people that you and I know. People don't know the meaning of life in general, and they don't know where they are going with their own lives.

What's the purpose of my life?

Actually, that is a terribly important question, no matter who you are and no matter what your age. It's the same whether you have lived many years or only a few. Life is precious, and we ought to know why we are alive and what our lives are all about.

It's especially important, however, for young men and women. Why? Because the evening of your life is determined by its morning. The end is shaped by the beginning.

It has been my experience that many people are simply enduring, rather than enjoying, their lives. They're just trying to get through. The favorite day of the week for these people is someday.

Someday their ship will come in.

Someday they will get that promotion or get that dream house or retire.

Someday they will find that perfect relationship.

Someday their prince (or princess) will come.

An astounding 94 percent of people who responded to a survey said they were simply enduring the present while "waiting for something better to happen."

The trouble is that life goes by quickly. And you can't let too many years simply slip between your fingers.

During the Christmas season, I heard someone sum up life like this:

1. You believe in Santa Claus.
2. You don't believe in Santa Claus.
3. You become Santa Claus.
4. You look like Santa Claus.

I'm pretty much in stage four right now. Old age already has its foot in the door.

The clock is ticking . . . for all of us.

Everything but Life

I heard a story about the great artist Michelangelo. Another artist whom Michelangelo knew had sculpted a beautiful angel and wanted the great master's opinion of his work. Michelangelo came over to his friend's studio and looked at the sculpture for a long time, studying it from many different angles.

Finally he looked over at the other artist and said, "It lacks only one thing." Then he walked out the door.

One thing? What was that one thing? What was missing?

The artist was terribly anxious to learn what his sculpture lacked, but he didn't want to ask Michelangelo himself. So he sent a friend to find out what Michelangelo meant—to find out what his sculpture was lacking.

Finally, Michelangelo revealed the answer. He said, "It lacks only life."

That could be said of a lot of people today. They have all the ingredients that most people suppose will make them happy: the ultimate house, the coolest car, the wealthy husband, the trophy wife, the seemingly perfect kids, a successful career, and money in the bank. They have everything that people normally associate with being satisfied and fulfilled.

But one thing is lacking. They lack life. It isn't physical life they lack, but that animating, energizing force that keeps a person on his or her toes with excitement, that thing that gets them out of bed in the morning.

But eventually we have to deal with death, too. And most of us don't plan on that. I'm reminded that the old rock group, The Rolling Stones, is touring again. Presumably they're still singing their old hit, "Time Is on My Side." Well, here's a note to Mick, Keith, and the boys: *No, it isn't!* That isn't gloom-and-doom talk; it's simple reality. It may come for you when you are old and full of years. Then again, it may sneak up on you and snatch you unawares. It doesn't matter whether you're old or young, rich or poor, famous or unknown. Death comes for all of us.

Facing Our Mortality

Bradley Cooper starred in the popular *Hangover* movies. He also was nominated for an Oscar for his role in *Silver Linings Playbook*. What's more, *People* magazine once named him "the sexiest man alive."

In an interview, Cooper talked a little about coming to terms with his own mortality. He'd been doing some thinking about death because of the recent passing of his father.

"Oh, right," Cooper admitted. "I'm going to die, too.

Here it is. It's not in a book. It's not in a movie. It's not in a story that was told to me. It's not driving by an accident or watching it on TV. It's someone you love dying in front of you. I was like, 'Okay. This is death. And this is going to happen to me one day.'"[1]

That's right, Bradley.

William Shatner, the original Captain Kirk in the *Star Trek* television series and movies, has been thinking along similar lines. Shatner has said, "I'm so not ready to die. It petrifies me. I go alone. I go to a place I don't know. It might be painful. It might be the end. My thought is that it is the end. I become nameless, and I spent a lifetime being known."[2]

Everyone has to face this. I had to face it as a young man. As far back as I can remember, I was searching for the meaning of life. It may have been forced on me earlier than most because of the home I was raised in. I had a beautiful mother, whom many people claimed was a dead ringer for Marilyn Monroe. She was married and divorced seven times, with a lot of boyfriends in between.

The fact is that I was never planned when I came into the world. I was the result of a little fling my mom had while she was in Long Beach. That made me what people call an "illegitimate" child. My mom always was trying to find fulfillment in relationships with men.

She also was a raging alcoholic. She would get fully drunk every night and pass out. I was just a young kid and had to take care of myself—and her, too. There was no father there for me.

Ironically, the very life I'd hated so much being a part of as a child became my life as well. As soon as I was old enough, I was out drinking and getting drunk with my friends. Then, when the whole counterculture came along, I started using drugs as well.

Even in the midst of all that drinking and partying, however, I knew that this wasn't the answer to life, that there had to be something more. Where was life? I knew that it wasn't in the affluent, boozy lifestyle of the adult world in which I had lived with my mom. I also knew that it wasn't in the social culture of my high school, with all the drinking and partying. It clearly wasn't in the drug culture either.

So where was the answer?

About that time, a cute girl came along. And not long after that, everything changed for Greg Laurie.

The Day It All Changed

She was attractive—not a beauty queen, you understand, but a girl who seemed pretty inside and out. There was something special about her that I couldn't quite identify.

I remember thinking, *Who is that girl?* When I saw her talking to a friend of mine on our high school campus, I thought, *This is my chance. I'm going to walk right up, break in on that conversation, and introduce myself.*

As I walked up and waited for them to stop talking for a moment, I noticed a book that she was carrying along with her notebook and a couple of textbooks. When I saw what it was, my heart sank a little. It was one of those strange books with gold-edged pages and ribbons coming out of the top: a Bible.

I groaned inwardly. *Oh no,* I said to myself. *A Jesus freak! What a waste of a perfectly cute girl.* I talked to her a little bit anyway, and then we went on our way.

For some reason, I couldn't get her out of my mind. During lunch hour that day, I wanted to see where she was and whom she was with. I found her sitting on the grass with a group of other kids, singing songs about God. I sat down far enough away so that people wouldn't think I was one of them, but close enough to eavesdrop a little.

I looked at those Christians with big smiles on their faces and thought to myself, *These guys are nuts. They're a few clowns short of a circus. There's something wrong with them.*

My problem was that I knew some of those people. Some of those guys used to be my buddies, and I knew how much they had changed.

Suddenly, I found myself trying an alarming new thought on for size: *What if it's true? Of course it COULDN'T be true, but . . . what if the Christians are right? What if Jesus Christ is alive? What if God can be known? What if I can change?*

Then I caught myself and said, *Oh no. There's no way, no chance for someone like me. Not with the life I've lived. I could never change. But . . . what if I could?*

Then came the day when I heard a preacher quote the words of Jesus from Matthew 12:30, saying, "He who is not with Me is against Me." I looked at the Christians sitting around me and thought, *Well, they're for Him for sure, and I'm not one of them. Does that mean that I'm against Him? I certainly don't want to be against Him!*

That was the day I put my faith in Jesus Christ. Believe me, it was the last thing I had planned on doing that day. And it also happened to be the greatest thing I have ever done.

A Story of Two Sons

There is a story from the Bible that you might think of as an Instagram from God. Or, maybe you could call it a selfie from the Lord. This is where the Lord says, "I'm going to tell you a story about Myself."

Some call this the story of the prodigal son. It's the story of a boy who ran away from home and how his father loved him, missed him, waited for him, longed after him, and prayed for him. It's the story of a young man coming home again in disgrace and being forgiven by his father for all the careless, heartless, and rebellious things he had done.

Bottom line, it's the story of you and of me running from God. Luke related the story in chapter 15 of his gospel:

> "A man had two sons. The younger son told his father, 'I want my share of your estate now before you die.' So his father agreed to divide his wealth between his sons.
>
> "A few days later this younger son packed all his belongings and moved to a distant land, and there he wasted all his money in wild living.

About the time his money ran out, a great famine swept over the land, and he began to starve. He persuaded a local farmer to hire him, and the man sent him into his fields to feed the pigs. The young man became so hungry that even the pods he was feeding the pigs looked good to him. But no one gave him anything."
(verses 11–16, NLT)

Let's think about this story for a moment. Here is a father with two sons. Obviously it's a nice, affluent home, complete with servants. The young man was deeply loved by his father, as we will see at the end of the story. This was an affectionate and loving dad.

When some people hear about a Father in Heaven, they might cringe a little, remembering unhappy years with a dad who didn't care for them. Maybe he was abusive and mean. Maybe he was distant and aloof. Maybe, as in my case, he wasn't there at all. Because of negative experiences in our past, we might get the idea of a God who is out to get us and wants to ruin our lives.

I heard a story about a man and a woman who had been married for over fifty years. A newspaper reporter went to interview them on their anniversary and ask them about the secret of their long marriage.

He interviewed the man first. "Tell me," he said, "how is it that you and your wife have been together for half a century? What's your secret?"

"Well," said the husband, "it really goes back to our honeymoon. We took a trip to the Grand Canyon. We were just getting to know each other in those days. I recall that we were riding mules down the trail into the canyon, and she was in front of me on a narrow path with a drop-off to one side. I noticed her mule stumble a little in front of me, and she leaned down and whispered something in the mule's ear. 'That's once,' she said.

"I wondered at the time what that was all about. We went a bit further, and the mule stumbled again. Once again she leaned forward and said something in the mule's ear. I heard her say, 'That's twice.'

"About a quarter mile down the trail, the mule stumbled a third time. She calmly reached into her purse, pulled out a 357, held it up to the mule's head, and pulled the trigger. Of course that mule dropped dead right there on the spot.

"I couldn't believe what I was seeing! 'That's horrible!' I protested. 'That's cruel! How could you do something like that?'

"She turned to me and said, 'That's once.' "

Sadly, this is how some people see God—as though He were up in Heaven just waiting for them to fail so He can throw a lightning bolt at them, frying them on the spot. "*That's once. You'd better not mess up again, because I'm out to get you!*"

Nothing could be further from the truth.

In the story Jesus told, the young man was sick of the rules, regulations, and expectations of living at home. The bright lights of the big city were calling to him, so this prodigal punk decided to get his share of the estate and get out of town. To divide such an estate, however, would have been very difficult. That was something that usually didn't happen until the head of the house passed away. But this kid didn't care about the grief, stress, or inconvenience he was causing his dad. He was saying, in essence, "Give me my inheritance now. You're going to drop dead one day, and I'm tired of waiting around. I want it now."

As we read the story, we're thinking this father should have said, "Not a chance, you ungrateful kid! You'll wait for the appropriate time." But this father let him do what he was determined to do.

In the same way, God has given you and me free will to choose our own path through life and toward eternal destiny. God says, "I love you and would love to walk through life with you and reveal the unique plan I have just for you. But if you want to turn your back on Me, you are free to do so." God won't force salvation down anyone's throat. He won't force anyone to go to Heaven.

If you want to, you can even choose to go to Hell. But that's the *last* thing God wants. The last thing the Creator wants is for any man or woman made in His image to spend eternity separated from Him in a place called Hell. Jesus died on the cross in our place and absorbed God's wrath for us so we don't have to face that judgment.

The father in Jesus' story let his son decide. In the same way, you can choose whether to believe or not believe. And in so doing, you effectively choose your eternal destiny in the process.

This boy wasted all of his money on wild living. He probably went to a first-century version of Las Vegas, because "what happens in Vegas stays in Vegas." At least that's what we're told. But would you believe it? When his money ran out, all his new friends simply disappeared.

I heard a story about two friends who went deep into the woods on a camping trip. As they were getting up in the morning for their first cup of coffee, they heard rustling in the bushes. Looking up across the clearing, they saw a grizzly bear running toward them. One of the friends immediately began lacing up his running shoes.

"What are you doing?" the other guy said. "You don't think you can outrun that bear, do you?"

"I don't need to outrun the bear," his friend replied. "I just need to outrun *you.*"

That's how it is with many so-called friends. When times get hard, they walk away. If you want to find out who your real friends are, put your faith in Jesus Christ and start following Him. You may discover that you don't have as many loyal friends as you thought you had. (But you will make new ones who will stand in the gap for you.)

This prodigal hit bottom. Have you had the experience of hitting bottom in life? Maybe you found yourself facing the consequences of your own actions. You got a DUI. You were arrested. You got your girlfriend pregnant—or, you are that girlfriend. You've gone through the breakup of a relationship or perhaps even a divorce. Maybe you've struggled with an addiction. That's how it was for this young prodigal. Even though he had been raised in a loving home, he took off on his own and hit rock bottom.

You may have been raised in a Christian home. You know all about *Veggie Tales* and Bob the tomato. But at some point in your life, maybe when you went to college or got out on your own, you turned away from the faith of your youth, and now you're living apart from God—and you're miserable. You have too much of the world to be happy in Jesus and too much of Jesus to be happy in the world. It's a no-man's-land. Here is what God is saying to you right now: "Come home before dark. Come home before it's too late. I will forgive you."

The prodigal son had been raised as a good Jewish boy but ended up feeding pigs, which definitely isn't kosher. So he went from living high on the hog to hanging out with the hogs.

That's sin for you! Sin promises a lot of things. It promises freedom, but it brings slavery. It promises success, but it brings failure. It promises life, but "the wages of sin is death" (Romans 6:23). It promises pleasure, but it ultimately brings misery and deep unhappiness.

Is there pleasure in sin? Of course there is. Even the Bible says so (see Hebrews 11:25). Sin can be fun for a little while. But all too soon, the consequences roll in. It might give you some euphoria to jump off the Empire State Building without a parachute. What a rush! Then bam! You hit the ground, and the fun is over—not to mention your life.

This boy finally realized, "I can't stay in this place any longer. I need to get out of here. I need to go home." He even prepared a little speech to deliver when he finally had to face his father. He told himself, *When I see Dad, I will say, "Father, I am no longer worthy to be called your son. Make me like one of your hired servants."* Thoroughly ashamed of himself, he began the long walk home again.

The text says that the young man "came to himself," or came to his senses. By the way, have you come to your senses yet? Have you seen that you need to get right with God?

We always have someone to blame in our lives, don't we? If there is trouble at home, we will say, "The problem is my parents." If it's at school, we'll say, "The problem is my teachers." If it's at work, we'll say, "The problem is my boss."

Sometimes someone will tell me, "Well, I came from a dysfunctional family."

Really? Give me a break! We *all* come from dysfunctional families. I came from a dysfunctional family, and now I'm the head of a dysfunctional family. *Deal with it.* Sooner or later you will have to accept responsibility for your actions and say three very important words: *I have sinned.* That's the beginning. You have to say from your heart, "I know it is my fault."

In Jeremiah 17:9–10 we read,

> "The heart is deceitful above all things,
> And desperately wicked;

Who can know it?

I, the LORD, search the heart,

I test the mind."

When the prodigal came to his senses, he basically said, "I'm not going to deceive myself any longer. I've been the problem from day one, and now I just want to go home—if Dad will have me." It had suddenly dawned on him that the very home he couldn't get away from fast enough was looking better all the time.

I read a newspaper article about a rich young heiress who had been raised in the very lap of luxury. She was dressing up for real by age ten with her first Chanel bag and was wearing snakeskin pumps by age eleven. At sixteen she had her own luxury car.

As she got older, she partied hard, drank hard, and did recreational drugs, according to her mother. She loved dogs and carried them around in her Hermes Birkin bag. Then the heiress adopted a baby girl. Later when she took her daughter to her father's estate to introduce the two, her father's then-girlfriend wouldn't let them in. But the heiress insisted, "This is my father's house, and I'm staying here until he gets here because I want him to meet my daughter."

The police were called, and when her father pulled up and saw his daughter, he told her to get off his property.

She had diabetes and needed to take insulin, but she reportedly ate junk food and took cold medicine to help her sleep. Then one night she tweeted her followers and

Facebook friends with what would be her last message: "Sweet dreams everyone . . . I'm getting a new car . . . Any ideas?"

She fell asleep and never woke up.

No matter who you are, no matter what your earthly father may have been to you, you have a Father in Heaven who loves you.

And once you open your life to Him, He will never, never turn you away from His house. Jesus said, "There is more than enough room in my Father's home. If this were not so, would I have told you that I am going to prepare a place for you? When everything is ready, I will come and get you, so that you will always be with me where I am" (John 14:2–3, NLT).

Your Father in Heaven will welcome you with open arms.

How Does the Story End?

Going back to Luke's gospel, we read in *The Message* version:

> "He was so hungry he would have eaten the corn-cobs in the pig slop, but no one would give him any.
>
> "That brought him to his senses. He said, 'All those farmhands working for my father sit down to three meals a day, and here I am starving to death. I'm going back to my father. I'll say to him, Father, I've sinned against God, I've sinned before you; I don't deserve to be called your son. Take

me on as a hired hand.' He got right up and went home to his father.

"When he was still a long way off, his father saw him. His heart pounding, he ran out, embraced him, and kissed him. The son started his speech: 'Father, I've sinned against God, I've sinned before you; I don't deserve to be called your son ever again.'

"But the father wasn't listening. He was calling to the servants, 'Quick. Bring a clean set of clothes and dress him. Put the family ring on his finger and sandals on his feet. Then get a grain-fed heifer and roast it. We're going to feast! We're going to have a wonderful time! My son is here—given up for dead and now alive! Given up for lost and now found!' And they began to have a wonderful time."

(15:16–24)

I love this story, this amazing self-portrait in God's own words. And I want you to notice something in particular: *The father accepted the son just as he was.* You've got to know that this young man didn't smell very good. His beautiful designer clothes were all in sweaty rags, and he'd been hanging out in the pigpen. You could probably smell him a mile away. Even so, this dad ran to his boy and threw his arms around him. He didn't stop twenty feet away and say, "Whoa! You'd better clean your life up a little, boy, and then we'll talk!"

The message here is that you need to come to God as you are. Come with your sins. Come with your problems. Come with your questions. Come with your doubts. Come with the broken pieces and shards of your dreams.

That's the way it was for me on the day I came to Christ. I still had a lot of doubts and questions in my mind. I even thought to myself, *This probably won't work for me. I'm not the religious type; I'm the cynical type.*

Very soon, however, I found out that God wasn't looking for a religious person. He was looking for a sinful person, and I qualified.

So do you. You don't need to clean up your life before you come to God. You need to come to God, and *He* will clean up your life.

I want you to notice something. The father *ran* to the son. In this day and time, it was considered undignified for an older man to run like that. It just wasn't done.

Running goes against all my natural inclinations as well. I've tried it, and I hate it. My runner friends say, "Hey man, hang in there, and you'll feel the release of the endorphins." It's never happened. I have never had so much as a single endorphin released. (Unless it was when I sank my teeth into my last cheesesteak sandwich.)

But this father hiked up his robes and sprinted down the road to meet his son. He was willing to lose his dignity to get to his boy as quickly as possible. By telling this story, Jesus was saying, "God loves you and runs to you if you will come to Him and admit your true condition."

But you need to get home before dark.

Why did I call this message "Home Before Dark"? When I was a boy, I lived for a time with my grandmother and my aunts, during the years when my mom was running around trying to find the meaning of life. When I would go out to play or spend time with one of my friends, my grandmother would always say to me, "Come home before dark."

And to tell the truth, I really wanted to come home on time because there always was a fantastic meal waiting for me. My grandmother made everything from scratch: fried chicken, mashed potatoes, black-eyed peas, and the best biscuits I've ever tasted.

Come home before dark.

You and I really have no idea when our last day or last moment on Earth might be. We don't know when life here will end. We don't know when that last opportunity to get right with God will come. It might be many years from now, or it might be today.

My hope and my prayer for you is that you will get home before dark, that you will come to Jesus or come back to Him as this message comes to a close.

My Two Prodigals

Like the father in the biblical story who had two sons, I am also a dad with two boys of my own. And just as in the Luke 15 story, both of my sons were prodigals. Though they were raised in a Christian home and taught to love the Lord from their earliest days, both of them went through a time of rebellion.

My oldest son, Christopher, always believed, but he just wanted to have fun. He liked to go to parties and soon began to experiment with alcohol and drugs. Though he had walked away from the way he'd been raised, he always knew that I loved him, and he always knew he could come home.

After many years of praying and waiting, my son Christopher did come back to the Lord. He made a recommitment to Christ, married a beautiful girl named Brittany, and they had a child together, with another one on the way. We were just loving this new life with our son as he served the Lord and took care of his family.

Then on July 24, 2008, my son was unexpectedly called home to Heaven, and that is where he is now.

Christopher's younger brother, Jonathan, also was going through a prodigal phase. As Christopher was ending his rebellion, Jonathan's was just getting started. Jonathan was struggling with drugs, just as his brother did. As brothers, they were close and would talk to each other about everything.

One day Christopher said, "Jonathan, what's it going to take for you to get right with God?"

Jonathan thought about that conversation and wanted to continue it with Christopher the next day. But the following morning, his brother died in a car accident on the freeway.

He never got to have that second conversation with his big brother, but he remembered Christopher's words to him: "*What's it going to take for you to get right with God?*" Jonathan made a recommitment to follow Jesus.

One day these bodies of ours will die, but our souls will live on. Because Jesus came, died for us, and rose again to life, we can have the hope and confidence that we will be reunited with our loved ones in Christ and be home with Jesus forever.

But you need to come home before dark.

Maybe you've never really had much of a home. No matter. You can come home today . . . tonight . . . right now.

Chapter 3

"GO AND SIN NO MORE"

Years ago when my son Christopher was a young teenager, he came home one day with a rat riding on his shoulder.

He had purchased his new little pal with his own money at a local pet shop. But that's all he had. Just a rat. He hadn't thought to buy any rat food or a cage. Christopher didn't think of things like that. He'd seen the rat, thought it was cool, and brought it home.

Cathe and I said to him, "Christopher, the rat needs somewhere to live. You've got to have a cage for him."

So Christopher got busy and built a very nice little house for his pet out of some balsa wood he had on hand. As I recall, he even put a name for the rat over the door of the little house. Christopher called him Nicodemus.

We all thought it was so cute. Nicodemus took up residence in his new little house that night, and we all went to bed.

The next morning, however, when Christopher went in to check on his new pal, the house was gone and the rat was just a little bit fatter. Apparently Nicodemus the rat ate his house.

Now why would he do that? It's because a rat is a rat. They don't think like we do.

Dogs don't think like us either. This will come as a revelation to some people today who treat their pets like they are people. Today we have pet psychiatrists, pet hotels, and even dog yoga. (Can you believe that? How would a dog even get into a lotus position?) Now we have people pushing dogs around in strollers. This has to stop! These dogs are kicking back, saying, "Yeah, I'm living the good life while people push me around."

Something's not right about this.

I read the results of a recent survey that said if given a choice, 40 percent of Americans would save their pet over a foreign tourist. Really? So your house is on fire, your dog is in there in one room, and a tourist is in another. And you're going to save the dog?

It gets worse. The same survey said that 37 percent would save their dog's life over an American they don't know. In other words, if I knew you, I might save your life before the dog's life. But since we haven't been introduced, sorry. I'm going to save Sparky, and you have to die today.

We've gotten things out of proportion. We treat dogs as though they are people. But a dog is a dog, a rat is a rat, and they're never really going to change.

But here is the question: *Do people change?*

Is Real Change Even Possible?

Is it possible for you to change or for me to change?

Most of us, to some degree at least, like the idea of change and living a different life than the one we're living right now.

Maybe you thought if you could move to a new place, you would change. Southern California, the area I call home, is a destination location for many people from around the world. Maybe you thought, "If I moved to Southern California, all of my problems would go away."

As The Mamas & the Papas used to sing, "I'd be safe and warm if I was in L.A."

But problems have a way of following us around, don't they?

Maybe you are single and have thought to yourself, *If I were married, I know I would be happy, because I'm so unhappy being single.*

Then you got married and found yourself thinking, *If only I were single again! I would be free—and then I would be happy.*

Then you were lonely again, so you gave marriage another shot and found someone else.

Maybe you had no children and thought to yourself, *My life seems so empty now. If we had some kids, I would be happy.*

Then you had children, and you told yourself, "I'll *really* be happy when the kids grow up and leave the nest."

Many of the life changes we think will bring us happiness actually don't. We find ourselves with the same old feelings as before.

Perhaps you've considered a change in your appearance, like a new wardrobe or maybe even cosmetic surgery. As we've all heard, Botox is very popular today. The problem is that some people put so much Botox in their faces that you really have no idea what they're thinking anymore. You might look at someone and say, "Are you really surprised to see me, or is that just the Botox talking?"

You've changed your appearance, perhaps, but you haven't changed a thing *under* your skin, where you really live.

Can We Really Change?

So can you change? Can I change? Can anyone change?

Here's the simple answer: Not really.

What I mean to say is that we really can't change ourselves any more than a drowning person can save himself. The Bible says, "Can a leopard take away its spots? Neither can you start doing good, for you have always done evil" (Jeremiah 13:23, NLT).

Some people will say, "Of course you can change. The answer is *within*."

Actually, the Bible teaches the opposite. God says that the problem is within and that the heart of the problem is the problem of the heart. In the book of Jeremiah, the Lord says, "The heart is hopelessly dark and deceitful, a puzzle that no one can figure out" (17:9, MSG). So each of us has to face the real truth that we can't change ourselves.

But I also have some good news for you: *God can change you.* He can make you a different person—someone brand-new—on the inside.

In the New Testament we read that "anyone who belongs to Christ has become a new person. The old life is gone; a new life has begun!" (2 Corinthians 5:17, NLT).

In My Own Life

After growing up in the chaos and heartache of an alcoholic home, I remember vowing to myself as a young teenager that I would never live like that. I would never get into a drinking, partying lifestyle. By the time I was in high school, however, I was doing the very things I had said I would never do.

But I also saw the emptiness of it all. I remember thinking, *I'm living this way, but this isn't right. This isn't how I want to spend my life!* When the drug culture came along, I got swept along in that, too. And it was just as empty as the drinking and partying.

For me, then, it became a process of elimination. *Where is the answer? What am I here on this earth for?* I knew that having money wasn't the answer, because I could see how unhappy my mother was. I knew that the answer to life wasn't in relationships because my mom had been married and divorced seven times, and I had seen failed relationship after failed relationship. I had tried alcohol and drugs, and I knew how empty *they* were.

Those were the kinds of things I thought about as

I walked around on the beautiful campus of my school, Newport Harbor High School in Newport Beach. I was a cynical young man with a hard heart.

But God had a plan to reach me, just as He had a plan to reach a cynical, burned-out woman whom Jesus met one day in an unusual way.

The Story of a Very Troubled Woman

The New Testament tells the story of the worst day in one woman's life. But that worst day ended up becoming the best day of her life after she had an encounter with Jesus.

Here's how it all unfolded:

At dawn [Jesus] appeared again in the temple courts, where all the people gathered around him, and he sat down to teach them. The teachers of the law and the Pharisees brought in a woman caught in adultery. They made her stand before the group and said to Jesus, "Teacher, this woman was caught in the act of adultery. In the Law Moses commanded us to stone such women. Now what do you say?" They were using this question as a trap, in order to have a basis for accusing him.

But Jesus bent down and started to write on the ground with his finger. When they kept on questioning him, he straightened up and said to them, "Let any one of you who is without sin

be the first to throw a stone at her." Again he
stooped down and wrote on the ground.

At this, those who heard began to go away
one at a time, the older ones first, until only Jesus
was left, with the woman still standing there. Jesus
straightened up and asked her, "Woman, where are
they? Has no one condemned you?"

"No one, sir," she said.

"Then neither do I condemn you," Jesus
declared. "Go now and leave your life of sin."
(John 8:2–11, NIV)

So here is a woman who had been caught having sex
with some guy who was already married. The religious
leaders who found her dragged her through town, hauling
her in front of Jesus, who had apparently been teaching in
the temple. They wanted to put her to death, but before
they did, they wanted to see if they could also use her in a
plot to bring down Jesus, whom they hated.

As I said, this must have been the worst day of her life.
She had been humiliated, perhaps betrayed, manhandled,
and dumped unceremoniously before the famous young
rabbi named Jesus.

It was a terrible day for this woman, a living nightmare
of a day. And yet . . . it became the best day of her life.

It all began, however, with her facing a charge of adultery, a capital offense in that day and time.

What Is Adultery?

I heard about a little boy who was in Sunday school and heard a talk from his teacher on the Ten Commandments. On that particular day, the teacher had focused on the seventh commandment: "You shall not commit adultery."

The little guy didn't quite understand it. Driving home with his dad, he said, "Dad, what does it mean when the Bible says, 'You shall not commit agriculture'?" He was just a little bit confused.

His dad, however, didn't miss a beat. He replied, "Son, that means you're not supposed to plow the other man's field."

The little guy was happy with that answer.

Adultery, of course, is being unfaithful to your wife or your husband. It's also called extramarital sex. The Bible also speaks of premarital sex and calls it "fornication." Both extramarital sex and premarital sex are classified as sins before God. In Hebrews 13:4 we're told, "God will judge the adulterer and all the sexually immoral" (NIV).

Someone will say to me, "Oh Greg, please give me a break. Sex doesn't hurt anyone."

Really? Have you ever heard of something called AIDS? Did you know that AIDS is the leading global killer of people between the ages of twenty-five and forty-four? Twenty-five percent of all HIV infections are found in people under the age of twenty-two. Sexually transmitted diseases like syphilis, herpes, and gonorrhea have reached epidemic proportions in parts of our world.

Sex doesn't hurt anyone? What about teenage pregnancies? Each year more than one million teens become pregnant. Many of these babies, however, never make it to term because they are aborted. One out of every five abortions is performed on a woman under the age of twenty. Four out of every ten teenage pregnancies end in abortion.

You don't think that hurts someone? I will tell you whom it hurts: the unborn children made in the image of God. Their life is ended. Thank God that our Father in Heaven welcomes these little ones who were unwanted by their earthly fathers and mothers.

It also hurts the woman who gets the abortion. According to one thirteen-year study, the suicide rate among women who had abortions was six times higher than those who had given birth in the previous year. As a pastor, I've talked to many of these girls who carry their guilt over taking the life of their unborn child for a lifetime.

That leads me to make this statement. If you as a woman end up getting pregnant outside of a marriage relationship, carry the child to term. *Have the baby.* If you don't want to raise the child yourself, put him or her up for adoption. There are many wonderful people who want to adopt babies today.

Please bear in mind that I'm not speaking from some ivory tower here. I was an unplanned baby and was conceived out of wedlock. My mom could have easily obtained an abortion, but I'm so grateful that she carried me to term.

It is a strange thing to discover later on in life that you weren't planned. So be it. Maybe I wasn't planned by my mom, but I was planned by the God of the universe. I've been in His plans before the beginning of time. In Psalm 139 we read these incredible, life-giving words:

> You watched me as I was being formed in utter seclusion,
>> as I was woven together in the dark of the womb.
> You saw me before I was born.
>> Every day of my life was recorded in your book.
> Every moment was laid out
>> before a single day had passed.
>
> How precious are your thoughts about me, O God.
>> They cannot be numbered!
> I can't even count them;
>> they outnumber the grains of sand!
> And when I wake up,
>> you are still with me!
> (verses 15–18, NLT)

We sometimes will call children born out of wedlock "illegitimate." But that isn't true. Every life is legitimate in the eyes of God. Everyone is loved by God. And He loves you in particular and has a plan for your life.

The Pharisees who caught this woman in the act of adultery didn't care a thing for her. Their hearts were so hard that they would have gladly seen her dead. But she was a handy tool in their hands at that moment because they wanted to find a way to trap Jesus.

They honestly thought they had Him that day. How could He respond? He might have said, "Stone her," as the Law required. But that would have been so heartless. If He said, "Let her go. It is no big deal," then someone would have thought, *He's disregarding the Law of Moses!*

The Pharisees thought they had Jesus stuck on the horns of a dilemma. Nevertheless, He knew exactly what to do. He used the incident as an opportunity to show God's forgiveness and mercy.

The Bible doesn't say much about this woman's background or character. She might have fallen into sexual sin for the first time that day. Then again, she might have had a reputation for being easy and sleazy. Either way, she was now facing the stark consequences of her actions.

What she needed in that moment wasn't a critic or a judge or the cold, curious stares of those who looked on. She needed a champion. She needed a rescuer. She needed a Savior.

Do you need to be rescued? Do you feel overwhelmed by situations in your life? Jesus is able to rescue you from your sin, from your addictions, and from your past. He did it for the woman in this story, and He will do it for you if you call on Him.

I love how this story develops. All of the accusers encircled Jesus and the condemned woman. They knew the Law of Moses, and the Law says to stone her to death. *But what do YOU say, Jesus?*

Instead of answering, He did what none of them could have ever predicted He would do. He bent down and began to write in the dust. What was He doing with His finger in that sandy soil? Making squiggles? Random lines? Tic-tac-toe?

No, I don't think it was random at all. I think what He wrote or drew was very significant, because after He had made one comment to them, they all began to drop their rocks and drift away, from the oldest to the youngest.

Maybe He wrote down something representing the Ten Commandments, making ten successive marks in the dirt. These guys knew those commandments backward and forward, and after each mark, He might have looked at one of the individuals in the group, getting eye contact and nodding His head a little.

Obviously as the Son of God, He knew everything there was to know about each of these guys. Did they sense that as He wrote?

Maybe He made some representation of secret sins that the men in that group thought no one knew about. The Bible tells us that "God will judge the secrets of men by Jesus Christ" (Romans 2:16). The psalmist says, "You spread out our sins before you—our secret sins—and you see them all" (Psalm 90:8, NLT).

John's account says the accusers left, from the oldest to the youngest. That's probably because the oldest guys had more to confess than the younger ones. Whatever the reason, all of the would-be rock throwers left after Jesus said, "Let any one of you who is without sin be the first to throw a stone at her" (John 8:7, NIV).

What do you think this young woman was thinking right then? She might have been saying to herself, *Oh man, I'm so dead right now! If these religious men couldn't stand before this man Jesus, how could I ever stand before Him?*

I love what happens next. He looked at her (I believe it was with incredible kindness) and said, "Woman, where are those accusers of yours? Has no one condemned you?" (verse 10).

"No one, Lord," she replied.

Chances are, she had been mistreated by men—used and abused—for years. She may have been made hard and cynical by men in her past. But she had never met a man like Jesus. He was holy, yet He was compassionate. She could see it in His eyes. And I'm convinced that she believed in Him right there on the spot.

How long does it take to become a believer? How long does it take to snap your fingers? That's how long it takes to believe. Just like that—in a flash . . . in a moment . . . in an instant. You find yourself thinking all of a sudden, *I get this. This is real. This is true. This is what I've been searching for.* Thoughts like those are the result of the Holy Spirit working on your heart and making things clear to you.

Jesus said to her, "Woman, where are those accusers of yours?" That word *woman* probably wasn't the word she was expecting. She'd most likely been called a lot of things in her life: hooker, whore, trash . . . but never *woman.* The word as Jesus used it was a polite term of respect. It would be like saying, "Ma'am," or "Lady." In fact, it's the same term He used to address His own mother as He hung on the cross. So He said to her, "Woman, *lady*, where are those accusers of yours?"

Why did He say that? She certainly hadn't been acting like a lady. No, but He didn't just see her for what she was in the moment; He saw her for what she would become. He knew that her life would change. He knew whom and what she would become as the years went by.

God sees the same in you right now—not just what you are or what you were, but what you can be when you put your faith in Him.

He said to her, "Go now and leave your life of sin" (verse 11, NIV). In the New King James Version He tells her, "Go and sin no more."

You might say, "That's kind of a tall order, isn't it, Greg?"

But He didn't mean that she would be sinless from then on. He meant that she needed to make a break with her past, make a change, and give her life to God.

Yes, He knew she would sin again. So will every one of us. All of us sin, stumble, and mess up. Every one of us falls short of God's righteous standards every day.

The Bible even says, "If we claim to be without sin, we deceive ourselves and the truth is not in us" (1 John 1:8, NIV).

Jesus was saying, "Lady, I don't want you to go on any longer in this lifestyle of sin. I want you to live a new life."

Sometimes people will say, "You know, God loves me just like I am." That is true. God does love you just like you are. *But He doesn't want to leave you that way.* He wants to change you.

With the woman's accusers gone and the crowd drifting away, Jesus gave this woman four strong assurances that are implicit in His remarks. In other words, she could walk away from the Lord that day with these comforting assurances ringing in her soul. And He makes those same four assurances to you and me.

Four Strong Assurances

1. HER SINS HAD BEEN FORGIVEN

Jesus said to her, "Neither do I condemn you."

Our God has a big eraser, and He wants to use it in your life right now. He will forgive you. But the Bible says that you must first confess your sins. In 1 John 1:9 we read, "If we confess our sins, He is faithful and just to forgive us our sins and to cleanse us from all unrighteousness."

The word *confess* means to agree with God. There are many times when we try to rationalize or justify our sins. We might say, "Everyone is doing this. It's not that bad. God understands. And I'm still a good person."

Are you truly a "good person"? If you are, then you're the only one on Earth. In fact, you are actually a bad person. Granted, some are worse than others, but according to the Scriptures, we are all sinners from birth. We aren't sinners because we sin; we sin because we are sinners. It's our nature.

To say that others are doing it and therefore you can

do it is *not* confession. That is not agreeing with God. To confess means to say, "God, You are right about that."

Stop making excuses for what you have done or said. Stop shifting the blame on others.

I'm reminded of the fact that even gorillas blame others. I read a newspaper article about a gorilla named Koko that had been trained to speak basic sign language. Koko was given a little kitten as a companion. The gorilla was actually delighted and treated the kitten with gentleness.

But then one morning Koko apparently got up on the wrong side of the bed and actually ripped the sink off the wall in her enclosure. (That's why you never want to get on the wrong side of a gorilla.)

When her keepers came in and demanded an explanation, Koko signed, "The cat did it."

God can forgive you of your sin, but it won't happen until you say the same thing about your sins that He does.

2. HER SINS COULD BE FORGOTTEN

God not only forgives, but He forgets.

The Son of God had forgiven this woman of her sins, and when God forgives, He puts our sins behind His back. In Jeremiah 31:34, God says, "I will forgive their iniquity, and their sin I will remember no more."

Here's the point: We should not choose to remember what God has chosen to forget. As Corrie ten Boom used to say, God takes your sins, throws them into the sea of forgetfulness, and posts a sign that says No FISHING ALLOWED.

Your sins can be forgiven, and your sins can be forgotten, no matter what they are, if you will put your faith in Jesus Christ as this woman did.

3. SHE WOULDN'T HAVE TO FEAR JUDGMENT DAY

Yes, as surely as the Bible is God's true word, there is a Judgment Day coming.

The Bible clearly tells us that one day, everyone who has refused to believe in Christ or receive God's provision for forgiveness will have to stand before the Lord in judgment (see Revelation 20:11–15).

But Jesus had said to the woman, "Neither do I condemn you." What an incredible word of encouragement! She didn't have to fear standing before God in her sin someday. And neither do we, if we have trusted Jesus as our Savior. It is so great to know that when you put your faith in Jesus and are forgiven, you don't have to be afraid of the coming Judgment Day. Why? Because God already has put His judgment on Jesus, who died in your place on the cross two thousand years ago. Christ paid the price for your sin so that you will not be held responsible for it. That is what He did for this woman, and this is what He will do for you.

4. SHE HAD NEW POWER TO FACE HER PROBLEMS

Did this woman still face problems and difficulties? Of course she did. And so do all of us. But when Jesus said to her, "Go now and leave your life of sin" (NIV), He meant that she now had the power to do that very thing.

She wasn't just "reformed"; she had been remade.

I'm reminded of what Paul wrote to the believers in Ephesus: "Work out the salvation that God has given you with a proper sense of awe and responsibility. For it is God who is at work within you, giving you the will and the power to achieve his purpose" (Philippians 2:12–13, PH).

Back to Our Question

Can people really change?

No, not by themselves. *But God can change us.* And He can do that for you right now.

The story of this woman in John 8 began with her being busted for adultery. Maybe you, too, have been caught in your sin. Maybe you have been busted or found out lately. Maybe you got pregnant. Perhaps you got a girl pregnant. Maybe you got a DUI. Or perhaps you were caught cheating, stealing, or doing something wrong. You didn't get away with it—you were caught in the act, as the woman in the story was. This woman was busted, but she turned to God.

Sometimes things like that can happen in our lives to get our attention or give us a wake-up call. Maybe you've had such a wake-up call in recent days. You had a close brush with death, and it got you thinking of your own mortality and the meaning of life.

That's a good thing. And if you are turning to Jesus Christ, it's the best thing.

4

GOD

IN PURSUIT

The last thing I ever planned on becoming was a preacher. Trust me when I tell you that. But when God became real to me as a teenager, I wanted more than anything else to share that with others—with people who were as cynical as I was, with people who had been raised in broken homes as I was, and with people who had been chewed up and spit out by the world like I was.

And please take my word on this: If God can use someone like me, He can use *anyone*. What's central here is not
the messenger but the message.

The message I am sharing is not original to me. I'm just
a delivery boy.

Years ago when I was a boy, I had a paper route. Today
you see adults delivering papers from their cars. But back
then, it was Greg on his bicycle. Bear in mind, however,
that this wasn't just any bicycle. It was a super-cool Sch-
winn Sting-Ray bike that even had a stick shift on it. (It
was sort of a forerunner to my Harley.)

I had canvas paper bags draped over my bike, and
I would throw editions of my hometown paper, the *Daily
Pilot*, onto front porches, getting as close as I could to the
front door. In time, I became pretty skilled at getting the
paper close to the door, learning how to clear hedges and
land it in the right place.

I was just a delivery boy. It wasn't my job to make the
news or write the news or edit the news. My job was to
deliver the news.

It still is. I'm still something of a delivery boy, simply
delivering God's message.

Someone might say, "Isn't that a little presumptuous,
Greg? Aren't you a little full of yourself in saying that you
are God's spokesman delivering God's message?"

No, it isn't presumptuous at all. If you are a Christian,
that's your job, too. In the New Testament, the apostle Paul
wrote, "So we are Christ's ambassadors; God is making his
appeal through us. We speak for Christ when we plead, 'Come

back to God!' " (2 Corinthians 5:20, NLT). God has called each of us to share the message about finding the meaning in life through Christ and how to get right with God.

Because He Loves Us

Years ago we were in a city in the midst of one of our crusades, and my family was staying with me at a hotel. My son Jonathan was very young at the time, possibly three or four years old.

He loved staying at the hotel because we let him push the buttons on the elevator. The little guy thought that was just the greatest thing: You would push a button and things happened. It would make a noise. An arrow would light up. And the doors would open, revealing an intriguing little room with still more buttons.

Jonathan loved this experience so much that he would always race ahead of me and push the right button. And that's where we got into trouble.

We were walking down the hallway of the hotel, and Jonathan suddenly sprinted out ahead of me, heading for the elevators.

I called out to him, "Wait for Dad, Jonathan! I'm almost there!" I turned the corner to see the doors of the elevator close, with Jonathan on board alone. Immediately I panicked, frantically pushing the button for the elevator to return. Finally the doors opened, but there was no one there. Jonathan had exited . . . somewhere.

I took the elevator to the lobby and ran up to the front desk. "Ma'am," I said to the desk clerk, "you've got to help me. My son is lost somewhere in this hotel! Please call security!" I was about ready to say, "And also call the fire department, the SWAT team, Delta Force, and the Navy Seals. You've got to help me find my son."

The clerk, however, didn't want to be bothered. She was on the phone. "I'm sorry, sir," she said. "Just hold on."

I had no time to waste. I had to find my son. I ran back to the elevator and pushed the buttons to every floor. As the doors would open on each floor, I would yell, "Jonathan! JONATHAN!"

Finally I found him on the fifth floor. He was just calmly standing there like he was waiting for me. I knelt down so that I could look into his eyes. Then I said, "Jonathan, listen to your dad. Don't do that again! Don't run off."

On that day, I was in pursuit of my son, and failure was not an option.

Did you know that God is pursuing you in the same way? He wants to pursue you to show you how much He loves you. Some of us have this warped concept of God chasing us down because He wants to give us some kind of a beating. Nothing could be further from the truth.

Some time ago, I heard the story of a lawyer who was trying to deliver an important paper to a man who was determined to avoid him at all costs. You see, this man assumed the attorney was trying to serve him with a subpoena.

He actually managed to avoid that lawyer for years. In fact, fourteen years passed and the pursued man was in a hospital, dying of cancer. One day he looked up and saw that they had rolled in the lawyer and placed him in the bed right next to him. He was ill as well.

The man looked at that lawyer who had been pursuing him for all those years and laughed out loud. "All right," he said. "Go ahead. Subpoena me."

The lawyer said, "Subpoena you? I was trying to give you a document that proved you had inherited forty-five million dollars."

That's a picture of you and me running from God. We think He's out to get us, when in reality, He wants to bless us.

A Man Who Ran from God

The Bible tells a classic story of a man who ran from God and how God pursued him.

The man's name was Jonah.

When you hear that name, what comes to mind? For many of us, it's the phrase "Jonah and the whale."

We all think of that whale, and because it involves Jonah's being swallowed by that whale—and surviving—we may dismiss this story as a fairy tale or a myth. But it isn't. It's a true story that was validated by Jesus Christ Himself.

At one point in the Lord's ministry, He told the religious leaders, "For as Jonah was three days and three nights in the belly of a huge fish, so the Son of Man will be three days and three nights in the heart of the earth" (Matthew 12:40, NIV).

In other words, our Lord would die on a cross, be buried in a tomb, and come to life again after three days. In making that statement, however, Jesus validated the Old Testament account of Jonah.

Actually, the Bible never mentions anything about a whale. It says that Jonah was swallowed up by a huge fish, though the technical translation would be "a sea monster."

I heard a story about a young girl who was out sharing her faith on a street corner, attracting a small crowd. There was a man standing in the back of this group who was an atheist, and he decided he would humiliate this young girl. So while she was talking about her faith in Jesus, he interrupted her and said very loudly, "Excuse me, young lady. I have a question."

"Yes sir?" she politely replied.

"You stand there and talk about the Bible. Do you *believe* the Bible?"

"Oh yes, sir. I do believe the Bible. Every word of it is true."

"Oh you do?" said the atheist with a little smirk. "Then you must believe the stories that are in the Bible."

"Yes, I do. I believe all of those stories."

"Oh really? So do you believe the story of Jonah being swallowed by a whale?"

"Yes sir," she said. "I believe that story. The Bible teaches that he was swallowed by a great fish or maybe a whale."

"Okay. Well, let me ask you this. Is that even possible?"

She said, "I don't know. When I get to Heaven, I will ask Jonah."

"Well," the atheist went on, "what if he's in Hell?"

"Well then, I guess *you* could ask him."

Anyway, we can be confident that the account of Jonah and the great fish (or sea monster) in the Scriptures is true because Jesus Himself accepted it as true.

Whales, Fish, and Other Creatures

When I was a boy, I had two aspirations. I wanted to be either a professional cartoonist or a pet shop owner. The cartoonist thing was really big for me, but the pet shop was my fallback plan.

I've always loved animals. It started when I was a kid, with my collection of reptiles. I had every kind of reptile imaginable: exotic lizards and snakes of all kinds. I had pythons, boas, gopher snakes, and king snakes. You name it. I had it.

Then I went into a small animal phase. I had rabbits, guinea pigs, mice, rats, and hamsters. Then I went into my bird phase. I had finches, parakeets, cockatiels, lovebirds, and a parrot. Then I went through my dog phase. I had a couple of poodles. (I was too young to know what I was doing. They were given to me.) I also had a collie, who was one of the dumbest animals that ever lived. Lassie would have been horrified. I went on to acquire a springer spaniel, two German shepherds, and a few nondescript mutts. One of those German shepherds, by the way, gets my vote for the greatest German shepherd of all time.

But I wasn't done yet. Then I went through my fish phase, with angelfish, oscars, and silver dollars. With all those animals, however, I have never had—or wanted—a cat. Why would anyone want a cat? When you call a dog, he comes running up to you and wants to play or give you a lick. What happens when you call a cat? He looks up at you as if to say, "Are you serious? You think I am coming to you? You're joking, right?"

I might add that I've also been *bitten* by many animals. I've been chomped by parrots, rabbits, hamsters, numerous snakes, and even a spider monkey that belonged to a friend of mine.

I'm looking forward to the day when Christ comes back and establishes His kingdom on Earth. In those days, the Bible tells us, the animal kingdom will be subdued. Isaiah 11:6 tells us that "the wolf will live with the lamb, the leopard will lie down with the goat, the calf and the lion and the yearling together; and a little child will lead them" (NIV).

I have even read stories of how animals have saved people's lives. Recently I saw that a dog managed to dial 911 when her master fell ill. Apparently the owner taught his dog, Belle, to bite his cell phone if he had a diabetic seizure, and that's just what the dog did. Another man I read about was saved by his dog when his SUV plunged forty feet down a ravine. He had backed too far out of his driveway, forgetting about the steep drop-off. He told his dog, Honey, "Go get help." The dog ran half a mile to a friend's house and brought back help.

These animals are so amazing. And in the story before

us, God used a creature to swallow the man who had tried to run from the Lord, essentially rescuing him from drowning at sea.

Someone might say, "There is no fish large enough to swallow a human being whole." But it doesn't matter if such a creature exists now. All we have to know is that it existed once. And it performed the task that God gave it to perform.

Man on the Run

The book of Jonah begins with a simple command—and a quick rebellion:

> Now the word of the LORD came to Jonah the son of Amittai, saying, "Arise, go to Nineveh, that great city, and cry out against it; for their wickedness has come up before Me." But Jonah arose to flee to Tarshish from the presence of the LORD. He went down to Joppa, and found a ship going to Tarshish; so he paid the fare, and went down into it, to go with them to Tarshish from the presence of the LORD.
>
> (1:1–3)

Have you ever tried to run from God? Maybe you imagined that God was out to ruin all of your fun and mess up your life. Nothing could be further from the truth. The Bible tells us that God is good. The Bible says, "Give thanks to the LORD, for he is good; his love endures forever" (Psalm 118:29, NIV).

God's plans for you are better than your plans for yourself. He says in Jeremiah 29:11, " 'For I know the plans I have for you,' declares the Lᴏʀᴅ, 'plans to prosper you and not to harm you, plans to give you hope and a future' " (ɴɪᴠ).

Jesus said, "I have come that they may have life, and that they may have it more abundantly" (John 10:10). In other words, Jesus is saying, "I came that you might have a life that is full, rich, and meaningful."

Meanwhile, the Devil wants the opposite for your life. Oh yes, there is a Devil. As surely as there is a God who loves you, there is a Devil who hates you and wants to destroy your life. Jesus said of Satan, "The thief does not come except to steal, and to kill, and to destroy" (John 10:10). Jesus, however, has come to give life because God is good.

But sometimes we don't understand that. Sometimes we run from God, the One who loves us most of all.

Two of our granddaughters and grandson have a little rabbit named Fuzzy. Every now and then they will pull him out of his cage to play with him. Little Christopher (named after his uncle) is only two.

Let's just say that he does not always hold Fuzzy in the right way. In fact, he thinks he should pick him up by his head, which isn't comfortable for Fuzzy at all.

"No, Christopher," we will say. "You have to support him when you hold him. See? Like this."

The other day when I was returning Fuzzy to his cage, he leaped out of my arms and into the open cage. It was as though he were saying, "Thank God! I'm so happy to be home!"

That is how we sometimes imagine life with God—like a cage with bars hemming us in. That's one way to look at it, I guess. But I think Fuzzy the rabbit would tell you, "Those bars are my salvation. Those are the bars that keep Christopher out. It's safe in here."

There are definitely areas that are off-limits for followers of Jesus Christ, commandments that were put there for our good, our protection, and our happiness. The purpose of these restrictions isn't to keep you penned in, but to keep evil out of your life. The Bible says, "No good thing will He withhold from those who walk uprightly" (Psalm 84:11).

Jonah Goes Down

Jonah ran from God, but it wasn't because he felt that God was withholding something good from him. As we will see, it was because God wanted to do good and show mercy to some people that Jonah hated.

Jonah had been called to preach to the people of Nineveh and warn them to repent from all their evil, violent ways. But Jonah didn't want to go. He didn't want God to even think about giving any mercy to these people. He was a patriotic Israelite, and the Assyrians of Nineveh were Israel's bitter enemies. It would be like God revealing to a modern Israeli that He was intending to judge the nation of Iran. But then, at the last minute, the Lord directs this Israeli to preach to the Iranian population so they might be spared: "Go to Tehran, Iran, that great city, and preach to them the message I give you."

I'm betting that Israeli would want to make very sure that he or she had really heard the voice of God correctly. The reason being is that the leaders of Iran have repeatedly called for the destruction of the nation of Israel.

More than just about anything else, Jonah wanted God to bring judgment against this hostile northern neighbor. In short, he wanted them to fry. That would be one less enemy that Israel had to worry about.

So when God said to Jonah, "Go to Nineveh," the prophet's response was essentially, "God, are You kidding? They drink *haterade* in Nineveh. I don't want to go."

In short, this is what happened.

God said, "Go."

Jonah said, "No."

God said, "Oh?" The Lord will always have the last word.

Historical records give graphic accounts of the cruel treatment that Nineveh gave to its captives. They would burn boys and girls alive. They would torture adults, literally tearing the skin from their bodies and leaving them to die in the scorching sun. Yet amazingly, God loved these people and wanted to give them a second chance.

So Jonah got up and went—*in the wrong direction.*

The Bible says, "But Jonah arose to flee to Tarshish from the presence of the Lord. He went down to Joppa, and found a ship going to Tarshish" (Jonah 1:3).

He went down.

That's where sin always will take you: down. We don't plan on going down, but one thing leads to another: that flirtation that ruined a marriage . . . that pregnancy that altered your life . . . that pleasure that turned into an addiction . . . the little, seemingly insignificant things that turned into big things.

Have you ever seen a little baby rattlesnake? They're actually kind of cute in a weird sort of way. Everything is miniaturized, from tiny little fangs to an itsy bitsy rattle.

You might say, "Look at that baby rattlesnake!" and try to pick it up.

Don't do it. Drop for drop, the venom of a baby rattler is superpotent.

In the same way we will say, "It's just a *little* sin. It's just this once, and I'll never do it again."

Nevertheless, sin's venom is strong, and little things have ways of turning into big things, as Jonah could testify.

I read about a rapper who found himself with a number one hit. In an interview, he talked about the aftereffects of his instant fame. His shows got bigger. His partying became more intense and extreme.

"I got more messed up than ever," he said. "All of a sudden, you're young, you have this newfound attention—I was hooking up with random females, and the drugs started getting stronger. I always said that I would never do coke, and I broke that. I started doing a little bit of OxyContin, which scared the [expletive] out of me."

His friends began to worry because he didn't respond to their texts and calls, and they assumed he was too cool for them. "But most of the time," one of them said, "I think he was alone, smoking in his bedroom."[1]

Sin takes you down. As someone once said, sin will take you further than you want to go, keep you longer than you want to stay, and cost you more than you want to spend.

Don't go that way.

The Storm

While Jonah was at sea, a storm came. But it wasn't just any storm. This was a big, frightening, epic storm. It was so scary and massive that even the seasoned sailors started to panic. They were used to rough seas, but they had never seen anything like that. Looked at from another direction, of course, it was a loving storm. God was allowing it to get Jonah's attention.

Maybe you've had a crisis in your life recently. Maybe you had a close brush with death or received a scary call from the doctor about some recent medical tests. Something happened to remind you of your mortality and the brevity and uncertainty of life.

Did you ever consider that God might be using such an event or circumstance to get your attention, speak to you, and show you your need for Him? C. S. Lewis once wrote, "God whispers to us in our pleasures, speaks in our conscience, but shouts in our pain: it is His megaphone to rouse a deaf world."[2]

Sometimes God can take pain, or a storm if you will, to get our attention and show us we need God.

Actor Gerard Butler, who starred in the movies *300* and *Olympus Has Fallen,* had a close brush with death recently. Learning how to surf big waves and prep for his film *Chasing Mavericks,* he got hammered by a wave and was pinned underwater for nearly a minute. Butler is an actor, not a seasoned surfer, and this incident terrified him. He thought he probably was going to drown. Fortunately, another surfer got to him in time. He was told that the last guy who went down at Mavericks had drowned, so he was fortunate to be alive.

After the incident Butler said, "You know how people say you get a sense of peace [when you think you're going to die]? I didn't experience that. It was violent."[3]

Yes, that can happen. And maybe it has happened to you.

Understandably, the terrified sailors on Jonah's ship were freaking out and calling on their gods to save them. The problem was that none of them had the right God.

When people are in trouble, they tend to cry out to God, even if they don't know Him. I'm reminded of an incident from my teen years. I was probably sixteen years old and was out driving around with some buddies. We bought a kilo of marijuana somewhere—not to sell but to smoke it all ourselves. We put it in the trunk of the car and went cruising down Pacific Coast Highway in Laguna Beach. It was raining that night, and one of my friends was driving.

Suddenly the car began to fishtail, and it felt like we were about to leave the highway. I was in the backseat, and it scared me to death. In a flash, I could see the headlines in the morning newspaper: "Drug dealers die on Pacific Coast Highway."

In those frightening moments, I distinctly remember saying, "God, if You'll get me out of this, I promise I will serve You."

Suddenly the car corrected itself, and we got home safely. In essence I said, "Thanks, God. See You next crisis."

Have you ever done that? "Oh God, if You get me out of this one, I promise I will follow You." Then, when He does just that, you forget all about that promise you just made.

Those men on the ship were crying out to their gods as best as they knew how, but it wasn't making any difference because none of them had the right God. Finally they figured out that the culprit was the stranger who was sleeping so soundly under the deck. It was Jonah, and they immediately woke him up.

By the way, that wouldn't be my chosen way of waking up, with the ship tossing around like a toy, the wind screaming, and a bunch of wet, frightened guys yelling at me.

Let's pick up the story in the Bible:

> They grilled him: "Confess. Why this disaster? What is your work? Where do you come from? What country? What family?"
>
> He told them, "I'm a Hebrew. I worship GOD, the God of heaven who made sea and land."
>
> At that, the men were frightened, really frightened, and said, "What on earth have you

done!" As Jonah talked, the sailors realized that he was running away from GOD.
(Jonah 1:8–10, MSG)

It blew them away when they heard that Jonah was a prophet of the God of Israel. They'd heard of God's fame. He was the One who parted oceans, rained food down from Heaven, struck the Egyptians with plagues, and raised the dead. So they were saying to Jonah, "Are you serious? Do you mean that you're running away from *that* God?"

Nothing is more pathetic than being busted by non-Christians—especially when they're right. Have you ever had that happen?

A non-Christian says, "Hey, I thought you were a Christian."

"Well, I am."

"Then why are you doing that? Why are you acting that way?"

"Umm . . . good question."

That happened to me years ago. I had become a Christian and had just started pastoring our church. At the time, I had shoulder-length hair and a full beard. I was sitting in a pizza restaurant, waiting for a friend, when I looked over at the table next to me and recognized a guy from elementary school. His name was Paul.

"Excuse me," I said. "Is your name Paul?"

He said, "Yes, it is."

"Paul, it's Greg Laurie!"

He smiled and said, "Man, I didn't recognize you under

all that hair." (If you've seen any recent pictures of me, you'll really have to use your imagination here.)

"Well, Paul, how have you been?"

"I've been good. How about you?"

"Good! You see, I've changed a lot, Paul. I've become a Christian. And not only am I a Christian, but I'm the pastor of a church."

He looked at me like I was crazy and then just shook his head. He said, "Greg, you always used to get in trouble. You were always smarting off to the teacher. You were always pulling pranks on other people. I can't believe you're a Christian, much less a minister!"

"Oh yes, I am. I am serving the Lord now, Paul, and you should too!"

Paul didn't seem to want to engage in the conversation, and he ended it by saying, "Okay, Greg. That's great. Nice seein' ya."

I was feeling so good about myself and that conversation. But as my friend and I ordered our pizza and spent some time catching up, I forgot all about Paul. When the pizza came, my friend was in the restroom, and I thought I'd play a trick on him. I thought it would be really funny to take the red pepper flakes and pour them all over my friend's side of the pizza so that when he took his first bite, it would burn his mouth.

So there I was, laughing and snickering and pouring red pepper flakes on my friend's food. From the next table, Paul looked over at me and said, "You really haven't changed much, have you, Greg?"

He was right. I hadn't changed nearly enough.

Sometimes we're like Jonah. We blow it in some area of our lives, ruin our testimony, and end up not being the representative of Jesus that we ought to be.

Some people might call that being hypocritical. It probably is. But every Christian in the world is going to be inconsistent in their lives. So if you're looking for a hypocrite-free church, please don't join it. You'll ruin it!

The fact is that Jesus did not say, "Follow My followers." He said, "Follow Me."

"Why Are You Running from God?"

The sailors were asking the groggy prophet, "Why would you run from a God like this?"

Sometimes nonbelievers have a better idea of what believers should do than some believers have. I read a true story about a bar that was being built in Texas. A local church started a campaign with petitions of prayers to stop it. Work progressed on the bar until a week before its opening, when it was struck by lightning and burned to the ground. The bar owner sued the church, claiming that they were responsible for the fire because of their prayers. The church indignantly denied any responsibility, saying there was no connection between their prayers and the fire that destroyed the tavern.

The case went to court. When the judge read the plaintiff's complaint and the defendant's reply, he said, "I don't know how I'm going to decide this, but it appears from the paperwork that we have a bar owner who believes in the power of prayer and an entire church congregation that does not."

The sailors were saying, "Why would you run from such a great and powerful God who has been so good to His people?" That's a good question. Why would you ever want to run from a God who loves you, wants to forgive you, and offers you a new life?

Under the Sea

Here is what happened next:

> Then they said to him, "What shall we do to you that the sea may be calm for us?"—for the sea was growing more tempestuous.
>
> And he said to them, "Pick me up and throw me into the sea; then the sea will become calm for you. For I know that this great tempest is because of me."
>
> Nevertheless the men rowed hard to return to land, but they could not, for the sea continued to grow more tempestuous against them. Therefore they cried out to the LORD and said, "We pray, O LORD, please do not let us perish for this man's life, and do not charge us with innocent blood; for You, O LORD, have done as it pleased You." So they picked up Jonah and threw him into the sea, and the sea ceased from its raging. Then the men feared the LORD exceedingly, and offered a sacrifice to the LORD and took vows.

Now the L ORD had prepared a great fish to swallow Jonah. And Jonah was in the belly of the fish three days and three nights.
(Jonah 1:11–17)

Jonah imagined that he might be ending his life in that moment when his body hit the sea, but he was in for a surprise. The Lord had a custom-made watercraft to pick him up out of the water.

Inside that fish, however, Jonah stubbornly refused to seek God or pray.

Why did God rescue Jonah with a fish? Because Jonah was a prodigal son, and God loves His kids so much that He won't easily let them go. He will pursue them to find them, just as I did with my little son Jonathan when he disappeared into the elevator.

Are you a prodigal son? A prodigal daughter?

What is a prodigal? It is someone who knows very well what is right and yet chooses not to do it. Maybe you were raised in the church, and everyone thinks you're a strong Christian. But you have been living a double life and putting on quite a performance. You aren't fooling God, and deep down, you really aren't fooling yourself. It's time to return to the Lord.

A Second Chance

As we read on in the book of Jonah, we find that the reluctant prophet (after three very uncomfortable days) finally turned to the Lord, repented of his rebellion, and agreed to do what God had asked him to do.

The fish may have repented of his action, too, because he vomited Jonah up on a beach, somewhere on the way to Nineveh.

I think that the first words of Jonah, chapter 3, are some of the sweetest in the Bible:

Now the word of the LORD came to Jonah the second time, saying, "Arise, go to Nineveh, that great city, and preach to it the message that I tell you." (verses 1–2)

This time Jonah obeyed the Lord's command and went to Nineveh. The text goes on:

So Jonah arose and went to Nineveh, according to the word of the LORD. Now Nineveh was an exceedingly great city, a three-day journey in extent. And Jonah began to enter the city on the first day's walk. Then he cried out and said, "Yet forty days, and Nineveh shall be overthrown!"

So the people of Nineveh believed God, proclaimed a fast, and put on sackcloth, from the greatest to the least of them. (verses 3–5)

The people of Nineveh did *what*?

They believed God's message—the whole city! And they began to demonstrate their sincerity with a fast and putting on sackcloth to show their sorrow.

Going back to Jonah 3:1, I love how it says, "The word of the LORD came to Jonah the *second time*" (emphasis added).

I have good news for you: God gives second chances. He gives third chances. And He gives fourth chances—and as many as you need.

What was Jonah's sermon that proved so successful? "Yet forty days, and Nineveh shall be overthrown!" That's not a very hopeful message, is it? That's not what you would call feel-good preaching. But in a way, it was hopeful. Why? Because God cared enough about these people to give them a warning.

Think of a parent saying to a child, "If you do that one more time, there will be punishment. Okay? Understand? I'm warning you one last time." Then, if the conduct continues, punishment follows, and the child learns that the parent really means it. (If you're a grandparent, there is no punishment. We just hand the kids back to their parents for them to handle it. Grandparents are all about filling their grandkids with sugar and then handing them back to their parents. That's our job to spoil our grandchildren.)

I do believe that God, in His love and mercy, gives warnings. Read the Old Testament prophets and see how Israel was warned time after time after time to put away their sin and turn back to God.

I believe God is warning our nation as well. He gives us chance after chance after chance to repent and turn around.

But there will come a time when He gives a last chance. And then He will bring judgment. I believe the only hope for our great country is to turn back to God and turn away from our sin. We need a spiritual awakening in the United

States again. We have had four great spiritual awakenings in our nation, and we are due for another.

God was warning Nineveh in Jonah's day, and He is warning America in ours. His message was and is, "Turn back to Me now."

I am no prophet and have never been swallowed by a fish. (Even though I've done my share of swallowing fish.) Nevertheless, I have a message for you. Here it is: There is only one hope in this life that can turn it around. There is only one lifeline that God has dropped from Heaven for us to be forgiven of our sins. It is His Son Jesus Christ, who was born in a manger, died on a Roman cross, and rose from the dead three days later. That very same Jesus now stands at the door of your life and knocks. If you will hear His voice and open the door, He will come in (see Revelation 3:20).

Jesus said it best in John 14:6: "I am the way, the truth, and the life. No one comes to the Father except through Me."

He is your answer and your only hope of salvation.

HIGHWAY

TO HEAVEN

I read about an extensive survey conducted by a leading polling agency. Questionnaires were distributed to people of various ages and occupations, and the key question was this: What are you looking for in life?

The pollsters were surprised by the answers. Instead of people saying their ultimate goal or ultimate purpose in life was to be successful or to make a lot of money, they found that the top three things people were looking for in life were love, joy, and peace.

Isn't that interesting? Young people, old people, middle-aged people—everybody is looking for love, joy, and peace. And interestingly, the Bible tells us that these three qualities are the fruit, or outcome, of having the Holy Spirit in our lives (see Galatians 5:22). In other words, these very things are the result of a life being changed by Jesus Christ.

But maybe someone would say to me, "Oh Greg, give it a rest! Love, joy, and peace? Get over it! People were talking about that stuff back in the 1960s—remember the 'Age of Aquarius'? And look where it got us! You aren't going to find love, joy, and peace in this world today."

There is a great deal more pessimism in the world today than when I was growing up. Many people—both young and old—have developed a dark, very cynical view of the world. Benjamin Disraeli, the former Prime Minister of England, came to this conclusion: "Youth is a blunder; manhood a struggle; old age a regret."

Or here is a quote from actor George Clooney. He says, "I don't believe in happy endings, but I do believe in happy travels, because ultimately, you die at a very young age, or you live long enough to watch your friends die. It's a mean thing, life."[1]

I'm here to tell you there is more to life than this. You *can* experience love, joy, and peace. There is something, or more to the point, *someone* to believe in who can give you those things. His name is Jesus Christ. He not only promises you life beyond the grave, but He promises you life during life.

As I've mentioned before, I became a Christian when I was a teenager, while being raised in a really strange home. As I've noted, my mom was an alcoholic, and she married and divorced seven times. So I was raised in this really bizarre environment and grew up with a huge distrust of the adult world in general. Again and again I saw what the partying, drinking lifestyle had done to my mom, and I determined that I would *not* go that way in life.

But I did anyway. As I got into my teen years, I was out partying and getting drunk with all of my buddies. And then after a while I thought, *Well, maybe that's not where it's at,* and I even got into drugs for a few years. I pretty much went out and sampled what this world had to offer. As the old cliché goes, I've been there, done that, and bought the T-shirt.

By the time I was seventeen, I started asking the big questions in life: *What is the meaning of life? What's going to happen when I die?* I wasn't just looking for life beyond the grave; I was looking for a life worth living on this earth. And then one day, someone told me about Jesus Christ and how He said, "I have come that they may have life, and that they may have it more abundantly" (John 10:10).

I want to tell you how to come into that relationship with God. He promises all of this if you will get on the road that leads to Heaven.

The Road

If we want to get somewhere on a road, the first thing we'd better determine is whether it's the *right* road.

If you're in Washington, DC, and you want to be in California, you'd better find a freeway running west.

In the same way, if you want to get to Heaven, you need to get on God's road. But where is this road? Is it hard to find? And is it hard to walk on once you've found it?

Here is what the Bible says in the book of Isaiah:

> And a great road will go through that once deserted land.
>> It will be named the Highway of Holiness.
> Evil-minded people will never travel on it.
>> It will be only for those who walk in God's ways;
>> fools will never walk there.
> Lions will not lurk along its course,
>> nor any other ferocious beasts.
> There will be no other dangers.
>> Only the redeemed will walk on it.
> Those who have been ransomed by the LORD will return.
>> They will enter Jerusalem singing,
>> crowned with everlasting joy.
> Sorrow and mourning will disappear,
>> and they will be filled with joy and gladness.
> (35:8–10, NLT)

In this passage God is giving us a picture comparing our relationship to Him with being on a highway or freeway.

Living as I do in Southern California, I know something about freeways. And one thing I know is that if you want to get where you're going, you'd better get on the right on-ramp and merge onto a freeway heading in the right direction.

When I was in England and Australia, I had to contend with roundabouts. We're getting more of those in the United States (but thankfully not so many yet). I remember being on a roundabout in England and I couldn't figure out how to get off the crazy thing. I made quite a number of circular trips before I finally found a way off.

Then of course in England and Australia, you're driving on the left side of the road—with the steering wheel on the other side of the car. That can be just a little bit frightening when you're not used to it. So there I usually find myself locked on a roundabout on the wrong side of the car going in the wrong direction.

Many of us are doing this in life. We're going in the wrong direction. We're going away from God instead of toward Him. And sometimes we feel like we're driving without a map, with no purpose or direction. Yes, we're moving, but where are we headed?

A lot of people are simply waiting for something to happen: waiting to get married . . . waiting to have children . . . waiting for their children to grow up and leave . . . waiting for next year . . . waiting for another time to take a long, dreamed-about vacation . . . waiting for retirement . . . waiting for tomorrow.

Does that describe your life right now? Are you just waiting?

If you're a preteen, maybe you're thinking, *When I finally turn thirteen, then I'm going to be happy.*

Or maybe you're a teenager, and you're saying, "When I get into my twenties, then I'll be happy."

Then you turn twenty-one, and you say, "Oh man, when I'm thirty and am out in my career and making a little bit more money, then I'll be happy."

But then you arrive in your thirties as single, and you say, "Everyone is getting married. I'll bet if I found someone and got married that I'd be happy then."

So you get married, and you find yourself (secretly) thinking, *This isn't working out like I thought. If I could just get a divorce and marry someone else, I know I'd still have a chance at happiness.*

So you divorce and marry again, but you don't have kids. So you say, "If we could just have a couple of kids, I think I'd be fulfilled and happy then."

So the kids come along, and you say to yourself, "These kids are driving me crazy. There's no peace. I'm so tied down. If we could just get these kids out of the nest, I know we would be happy."

And you always find that whatever it is you seem to be looking for is just beyond your reach. You're never quite there. And then, before you know it, the years have sped by, and there's more life behind you than there is in front of you. It's a bit of a cliché, but you've climbed the ladder of success only to find that it was leaning against the wrong wall. And you've been going nowhere in life.

But God has put before us the road to Heaven and the way that we can know Him, the very One who created us and designed us.

I realize that we can go a long time without thinking about these "big questions" of life. But then something gets our attention. Sometimes it's when someone close to us dies unexpectedly. It might be a grandparent or maybe a dad or mom who dies before anyone expected them to.

Or even more shocking, someone your age or even younger than you gets sick or gets in an accident, and suddenly they're gone. They've left this earth. That shocks you a little and makes you think, *If someone like that could die, it could happen to me as well.*

Most of us are uncomfortable even thinking about death. The statistics, however, are pretty impressive: One out of every one person will die. No one will escape it!

There's an old tombstone in Indiana inscribed with these words:

Pause, stranger, when you pass me by:
As you are now, so once was I.
As I am now so you will be.
So prepare for death and follow me.[2]

Someone reading that inscription is said to have added the following:

To follow you I'm not content
Until I know which way you went.[3]

Do you know which way you are going in life? Do you know which road you're on? Let's talk a little bit about this road to Heaven. There are five things we will discover in the pages of the Bible.

1. THERE IS A ROAD TO HEAVEN

Jesus said, "You can enter God's Kingdom only through the narrow gate. The highway to hell is broad, and its gate is wide for the many who choose that way. But the gateway to life is very narrow and the road is difficult, and only a few ever find it" (Matthew 7:13–14, NLT).

It's popular today for people to say that all roads lead to God. In one sense that's true. Whatever you believe, if you are a Christian, not a Christian, or even an atheist, you will get to God one day. You will stand before Him on the day of judgment.

You'll notice that I didn't say all roads lead to Heaven, because they don't. I said all roads lead to God, because the Bible teaches that one day, everyone will stand before God. Young and old, rich and poor, famous and unknown, everyone will stand before God one day to give an account of their lives. But there is only one road that will lead us to Heaven.

Jesus says that it's a narrow road. In other words, it's not necessarily the most popular road, but it is a road to Heaven and a way to a relationship with God.

Every day when I get up in the morning, I decide what path I am going to take and how I'm going to live. God says in Deuteronomy 30:19, "I have set before you life and death, blessings and curses. Now choose life, so that you and your children may live" (NIV).

Jeremiah 6:16 says, "Stand at the crossroads and look; ask for the ancient paths, ask where the good way is, and walk in it, and you will find rest for your souls" (NIV).

So I have a choice: I can walk down the road that leads to life, or I can walk down the road that leads to death. I can walk down the right path, or I can walk down the wrong path. I can take the road to Heaven, or I can take the road to Hell.

2. IT IS EASY TO FIND

I don't know about you, but I've always been navigationally challenged, which is a nice way of saying that I get lost quite a bit.

It's especially challenging for me when I'm in a place where I've never been before. I get turned around so easily. What a relief it is to know that God's road is easy to find. It's not hard to discover. I believe that Jesus Christ will reveal Himself and the way to God to any true seeker.

God Himself has said in the Scriptures, "I love those who love me, and those who seek me find me" (Proverbs 8:17, NIV).

God wants to show you the way to a relationship with Him. And if you really want to know it, you will find it.

3. IT IS A HOLY ROAD

Verse 8 of Isaiah 35 says, "It shall be called the Highway of Holiness." And then it says also, "Evil-minded people will never travel on it" (NLT). The Bible says, "Without holiness no one will see the Lord" (Hebrews 12:14, NIV).

What in the world is "holiness"?

Someone might say, "That sounds so unattainable. Maybe Mother Teresa was a holy woman, or some other people might be holy, but how could someone like me ever live a holy life?"

The answer is that you can't—not on your own. There is no way in your own strength that you can live the life that God requires because you will fail over and over again. You will falter. You will fall. You will come up short.

Maybe you go to church every Sunday and try to live by the Ten Commandments. You sincerely try to do the right thing, but you find that you keep on doing the wrong thing. And it's frustrating to you. So when you hear there is this holy road that God wants you to walk and this holy road that He wants you to travel on, you say, "Forget it! There's no way in the world that I could pull that off."

Again, that's true. You can't pull it off on your own. But the Bible says, "I can do all things through Christ who strengthens me" (Philippians 4:13).

When Jesus Christ comes and lives in your heart, He changes your desires. The things you used to long for don't have the appeal they once had. And the things you really had no interest in at all suddenly become the most appealing of all. Your whole worldview changes. Your outlook changes because your heart has changed. And only Jesus Christ can give you the righteousness and holiness that God wants. Because all of us have sinned.

But more than two thousand years ago, Jesus—the only one who has lived a perfect life—went voluntarily to a cross and died for the sin of the world. As a result of what He did, what He accomplished, when I turn from my sin and put my faith in Jesus, God forgives me of every wrong I have ever done.

Just think about that for a moment.

Think of all of the wrongs you have done—as far back as you can remember. Think of all the sins you have committed. Think of all the things you have done wrong that you wish you had not done and all the things you should have done but didn't do. God is saying in His Word, "Their sins and lawless acts I will remember no more" (Hebrews 10:17, NIV).

This just gets more and more amazing. God not only forgives your sin, but He also *forgets* your sin. He willingly chooses to remember it no longer, and that should be enough to blow our minds right there. But there's more.

Not only does God forgive you of your sin, but when you become a Christian, He also deposits His righteousness into your spiritual bank account.

Let's imagine that you got a credit card. Let's further imagine that you are sixteen years old and that you have never had a credit card before. So you got a little carried away and basically ran up one million dollars in debt. You realized there was no way you could ever repay this debt, and you were arrested and about to be taken off to prison.

Now let's imagine that Rupert Murdoch, a very wealthy communications tycoon, happened to be reading the newspaper and heard of your story. So Murdoch decides that he will settle your account. Calling up your credit card company, he pays your debt, and your balance with them goes from a million dollars to zero!

While you are still recovering from that wonderful shock, he calls you at home and says, "I would recommend that you go down and check out your balance in your bank account because I put a little extra money in there for the future."

You check your account, and now you have a new shock to absorb. Not only has Murdoch wiped out your debt, but he also has placed ten million dollars into your account!

Now that may all sound like a happy fairy tale, but it really doesn't even approach the reality of what Jesus has done for you. Not only has He forgiven you of all your sins, but He also has placed His own positive righteousness into your spiritual bank account. As the apostle Paul stated it, "God made him who had no sin to be sin for us, so that in him we might become the righteousness of God" (2 Corinthians 5:21, NIV). As a result, you *can* walk on this holy road that God has called you to walk on.

Some hear the word *holy* and think it must describe a life that is dull, boring, and vanilla. When many people think of the narrow way that leads to life, when they think of following Jesus, they picture a life of misery and restriction, rules and regulations. But the very opposite is true. If you still don't understand what it means to live a holy life, try respelling the word. It may help. To be *holy* means you live a *wholly* committed life in following Jesus Christ.

4. IT IS A HAPPY ROAD

We read these words a little earlier from Isaiah 35:10:

And those the LORD has rescued will return.
They will enter Zion with singing;
    everlasting joy will crown their heads.
Gladness and joy will overtake them,
    and sorrow and sighing will flee away. (NIV)

Notice it says that "gladness and joy will overtake them" on that road. That's quite a picture. It's like being at the ocean with your back to the sea, and suddenly a wave comes up behind you and just flattens you. Only in this case, gladness and joy will overtake and wash over those who are walking with the Lord. There is an indescribable joy that you experience in Christ.

Every day we see people go out looking for fun, looking for excitement, looking for fulfillment, and looking for a little happiness. Yet what the world has to offer is so temporary, vanishing away almost as soon as it comes. People will say, "If I could just have sex with this person, I know I'd be happy." Or maybe, "If I just tried this drug, it would make me forget all my problems."

Maybe you are experimenting with drugs right now, and no one knows about it except you and a few others. You are trying to fill a hole in your heart that can't be filled with drugs—or sex or partying or alcohol. It can't be filled with the things that this world offers. It is a hole in your heart that was created to be filled with God Himself through a relationship with Jesus Christ.

Which brings me to my last point.

5. IT IS THE ONLY ROAD TO LIFE

The Bible tells us, "There is salvation in no one else! God has given no other name under heaven by which we must be saved" (Acts 4:12, NLT).

Now I know that is hard for some people to accept because they believe that as long as you are *sincere* in what you believe, you will get to Heaven, and that it doesn't really matter what your specific beliefs are. They will say, "I don't care what the Bible says. I want to chart my own course, find my own road, and do my own thing. God will understand."

What God understands, however, is that you are lost forever, apart from the offer of salvation and eternal life in His Son, Jesus.

In the book of Proverbs, Solomon wrote, "There is a way that seems right to a man, but its end is the way of death" (14:12). Another version puts it like this: "Before every man there lies a wide and pleasant road that seems right but ends in death" (TLB).

Figuring out your own way to Heaven—borrowing a little from this religion and that religion and some of your own philosophy—may seem like a wide and pleasant road to you or your friends. But it is the wrong road, and it leads to a terrible dead-end.

Let me be really straight with you. Not only is there a highway to Heaven, but there is also a highway to Hell. To get on the highway to Heaven requires a choice and a decision. To get on the highway to Hell means basically doing whatever feels good to you in the moment and basically doing "what everybody else is doing."

Again, to come back to the words of Jesus, "You can enter God's Kingdom only through the narrow gate. The highway to hell is broad, and its gate is wide for the many who choose that way. But the gateway to life is very narrow and the road is difficult, and only a few ever find it" (Matthew 7:13–14, NLT).

Which road are you on? Because you *are* on one. You are either on the road to Heaven, the highway to Heaven, or you are on the highway to Hell.

You are the one—the only one—who can make this decision.

HOW TO FIND

ETERNAL LIFE

I heard a story about a man who was desperate for a job and heard they were hiring at the local zoo. Waiting his turn for an interview, he was finally ushered into the human resources office.

The man behind the desk said, "Hey, I'm really sorry, but that opening we advertised already has been filled."

Trying to hide his discouragement, the man mumbled a word of thanks and started for the door.

"One minute!" the zoo official said. "There might be something. You know, you're a good-sized guy. So . . . what I'm about to say might offend you, but I hope it doesn't. I want to make a proposition to you."

"All right," said the man, wary but interested. "What is it?"

"Unfortunately," the official said, "our gorilla died the other day. Now, we have one on order, and we're expecting him any day. Please don't be offended by this, but . . . would you be willing to put on a gorilla suit and pretend to be our gorilla until the real one arrives? We're prepared to pay you well."

Actually, it was more money than the man had even been hoping for. He shrugged his shoulders and said, "Well, it's not something I'd want to put on my résumé, but I do need the work. I guess I'll do it."

He showed up at the zoo the next morning, and they custom fitted him with a very realistic gorilla suit. He felt a bit foolish ambling into the enclosure and pretending to be an ape, but after a while he started to get into it. What amazed him was to find that the people were eating it up. The children were loving it, and the crowds were getting bigger and bigger by the day. So by day three he was beating on his chest and putting on a big show. By day four he was swinging on the vines and was actually beginning to enjoy the job. On day five, however, he got a little carried away with the vine swinging and went right over the wall and landed in the middle of the lion's den.

So now he had a dilemma. Would he reveal that he was just a man in a gorilla suit and get help? Or, would he risk being eaten alive by the lion? Looking over his shoulder, he saw the lion staring at him and beginning to walk in his direction. All the people watched breathlessly as the lion backed up the would-be gorilla into a corner.

Finally in desperation, the man in the gorilla suit cried out, "HELP!"

"Shut up," said the lion, "or you'll get us both fired!"

The moral of my little story is that things aren't always as they appear. There are people whom we see in movies or on television, celebrities from the entertainment world or sports who seem to have it all together. They're good-looking, beautifully dressed, drive cool cars, and live in wonderful houses. We see them and think to ourselves, *Man, they are living the good life.*

Maybe. And then again, maybe not.

Deep down, everyone has to deal with hurts and disappointments and empty, aching places in the soul.

Maybe you have found yourself thinking, *If I could become rich and famous, then I would be happy.* In an interview, rapper Eminem made this statement about his fame and fortune: "You gotta be careful what you wish for. I always wished and hoped for this. But it's almost turning into more of a nightmare than a dream. . . . I can't even go [out] in public anymore. I've got the whole world looking at me. I can't be treated like a regular person anymore."[1]

Singer Lana Del Ray has certainly had her share of fame at the age of 27. She shot to the top and has been very successful in her career. In a recent interview, however, she revealed that she hadn't felt any pleasure from fame in the three years she's been in the spotlight. She explained, "I never felt any of the enjoyment. It was all bad, all of it."

She has said that her life is like "a really [expletive] movie," and she's adamant that she doesn't want to live anymore. Ironically, she released an album back in 2012 entitled, "Born to Die." Then she made this shocking statement: "I wish I was dead already!" In an interview she admitted that she sees dying young as glamorous.[2] She has her beauty, her fame, her money, and amazing opportunities, and she wants to die.

Be careful of what you wish for!

I heard about a couple that was celebrating their thirty-fifth wedding anniversary as well as the husband's sixty-fifth birthday. Suddenly a genie appeared and offered each of them one wish.

The husband said, "*One* wish? Whatever happened to three wishes?"

"Times are hard," the genie explained. "We've had to cut back. You get one wish each."

So that wife looked at her husband whom she loved and adored, the man she had been married to for thirty-five years, and she made this wish: "I wish that my husband and I were having a second honeymoon on a beautiful island in the middle of the Bahamas."

And *poof*, there they were under a palm tree on a wonderful postcard island, surrounded by turquoise water.

The genie then said to the husband, "All right. Now, what would *you* like?"

He looked over at his wife of thirty-five years and said, "I would like a wife thirty years younger than me."

Poof. Just that quickly, he was ninety-five years old.

Be careful what you wish for. You might get it.

In this message we'll be looking at a man whose friends must have thought he had it all. Those same friends might have wished again and again that they could somehow trade places with this man. But that's because they didn't know the whole story.

A Man Who Had It All

The Bible tells the story of a man who was thought to have it all. He was rich, famous, and powerful. On the outside he looked good. He was a ramrod-straight military man, a general, a war hero, and a leader of men.

General Naaman the Syrian had a tough-guy reputation and could back it up. He was battle-hardened with nerves of steel. He was what we call a man's man.

Naaman must have been just about the most envied guy in Syria. He had power, military rank, and was second only to the king in authority. He had fame, making him a legend in his own time, and he was loved by the people and the king.

Because of these things, we can imagine that he had great wealth in keeping with his position. He probably wore custom-made, gleaming armor and drove the latest chariot. He seemingly had everything.

But he also was a bitterly unhappy man.

That's how it is for many people today. They have everything that our culture has decided should make a person happy, but they're not. Something isn't right.

And so it was for Naaman. Beneath that gleaming armor of the great general of the Syrian armies, something was amiss. Naaman had a career-busting, life-threatening problem that all of his money and power and fame couldn't fix. Naaman had leprosy.

Nowadays leprosy is called Hansen's disease, and it is treatable. But back in these days, it was not treatable. If you found out that you had leprosy, it was almost the same thing as a death sentence. Contracting leprosy must have been everyone's worst nightmare. The disease was disfiguring to the extreme and would cut you off from everything you knew and loved, essentially making you an outcast and a social pariah. You would never be allowed to have any physical contact with anyone anywhere. When someone with leprosy was walking down the street, he or she would have to cry out, "Unclean! Unclean!" so that people could clear the way for them, keeping them at a distance.

Leprosy was so disfiguring because people would lose their sense of touch. You could burn yourself and not know it. A vermin could eat a finger while you were asleep at night, and you would not be aware of it.

No one wanted to get leprosy or be anywhere near it.

But Naaman had it.

As it turns out, a young Israelite girl worked in his home. Actually, the girl was a slave who had been abducted on a raid from Israel. And when she heard that her master had leprosy, she basically said, "You need to go to Israel, and you need to look up the prophet Elisha. He is a very powerful man of God, and he will pray for you and God will heal you."

How easily this young girl could have taken perverse pleasure in his misfortune. But instead she told him he needed to go and meet the prophet Elisha.

Well, Naaman must have thought, *why not?*

He had run out of ideas, and there were no solutions or cures on the horizon. And so he made the trip. He got his entourage together, put together a military escort, put on his best uniform, and made the trip to Israel to meet the prophet.

In his mind, this proud man had to be thinking, *Surely these Israelites will greet me with honor and give me a good reception.*

And that's where we pick up the story in the Old Testament book of 2 Kings.

At the Prophet's Door

So Naaman went with his horses and chariots and waited at the door of Elisha's house. But Elisha sent a messenger out to him with this message: "Go and wash yourself seven times in the Jordan River. Then your skin will be restored, and you will be healed of your leprosy."

But Naaman became angry and stalked away. "I thought he would certainly come out to meet me!" he said. "I expected him to wave his hand over the leprosy and call on the name of the LORD his God and heal me! Aren't the rivers of Damascus, the Abana and the Pharpar, better than any of the rivers of Israel? Why shouldn't I wash in them and be healed?" So Naaman turned and went away in a rage.

But his officers tried to reason with him and said, "Sir, if the prophet had told you to do something very difficult, wouldn't you have done it? So you should certainly obey him when he says simply, 'Go and wash and be cured!' "

(2 Kings 5:9–13, NLT)

I love this story because General Naaman, who was so full of pride—so full of himself—felt like he'd already lowered himself to come to the prophet's door, hat in hand, so to speak, to ask for his help. He was expecting Elisha to come out to greet him (probably bowing low) and just wave his hand over him and heal him.

It's like a study in contrasts. There was Naaman in his beautiful chariot—he'd probably had it lowered, with spinning wheels and everything chromed out to the max. He came cruising into town with the sun glinting off his armor, his helmet, and his chariot. He expected Elisha to come out and greet him like a foreign dignitary, which he certainly was.

But at first no one even answered the door. Finally a servant named Gehazi answered. In my imagination, I see the door hanging by one hinge and in need of paint. Without any pleasantries or polite small talk, the servant abruptly told the general, "Go and wash yourself seven times in the Jordan River."

Then the door closed.

Naaman couldn't believe it. He was saying, "And that's it? That's all the consideration I am to be given? What's with this? Doesn't this Hebrew prophet know that I'm a great man? Why didn't he do a great thing for me?"

The Bible, however, says that we need to humble ourselves in the sight of the Lord. It isn't easy. It isn't convenient. It doesn't come naturally. It's hard to admit that you are a sinner in need of a Savior. It's hard to admit that you need God, or anything, especially for some men. Why? Because men like to fix stuff. We like to be in control. You tell us the problem, and we're going to resolve it. We'll take care of it and make it right. We don't like to reveal weakness—only strength. That's the way most of us are.

It's difficult for a man, or sometimes even a woman, to admit, "I need God. I need help."

But why did a strong, important military man like Naaman need help? Because he had run into something that was totally beyond his experience or expertise. He knew about armies and soldiers, swords, spears, and arrows. But he didn't know a thing about leprosy.

Suddenly all his wisdom and confidence and experience counted for nothing. One day he had probably noticed a little spot on his hand and thought, *Where did that come from? Maybe it's a scratch from that recent battle.* Then there was a spot on his other hand. Then there was one on his shoulder. Before long, a spot appeared on his chest—and then on his thigh. And it began to concern him. He couldn't shove it out of his thoughts anymore.

So he finally went down to see the doctor, and the doctor said, "General Naaman, after carefully inspecting you, I'm sorry to tell you this, but you have leprosy."

As stated previously, it was a death sentence. And you not only were going to die, but you were going to die a slow, painful, disfiguring, deeply humiliating death.

God was tapping on the shoulder of the famous general.

Maybe something like that has happened to you recently. You felt as though you were finally getting your life together and firing on all cylinders. Everything was rolling along smoothly.

But then the doctor called you after your checkup and said, "You need to come in. We need to talk." It certainly has your attention.

Maybe you've been involved in an accident or a tragedy or something out of the ordinary that's been like a wake-up call to you.

Maybe you've been let go from your job—or have been working at a job that pays much less than you need.

Maybe your marriage has gone south or one of your kids has gone sideways.

It could be that God is speaking to you. It could be that He's trying to wake you up and get your attention.

That's what was happening in the life of Naaman. He was finding out that it was time—and past time—to wake up and smell the coffee. It was time to face reality and realize that life wasn't going to last forever.

You may have just become more aware of the fact that

you are aging. Maybe you've passed a milestone birthday: thirty, forty, fifty, or beyond. Back when I was fifty-six, I found out that I could declare myself a senior citizen and get discount movie tickets. I've been taking full advantage of that situation, but at first it rocked me back on my heels a little. *Me? A senior citizen?*

Then there are all those telltale signs that time is catching up with you. You know you're getting older when you actually look forward to a dull evening at home. You know you're getting older when you sit down in a rocking chair and can't get it started. You know you're getting older when your mind makes commitments that your body can't keep. You know you're getting older when everything hurts, and what doesn't hurt doesn't work. You know you're getting older when someone calls you at 9:00 a.m. and asks, "Did I wake you?" You know you're getting older when you have owned clothes so long that they have come back into style—twice.

A number of years ago, Billy Graham was asked what had been the greatest surprise of his life.

His answer was, "The brevity of it."

So Naaman knew that life was coming to a close. He knew that he wasn't going to live forever. And deep down inside, we are all the same, whatever our age, race, gender, or culture.

Let me tell you a few things I know about you without even meeting you. (I know these things because they're true of all people, anywhere in the world.)

Four Things I Know about Everyone

1. THERE IS AN EMPTINESS IN EVERY PERSON'S LIFE WHO DOESN'T KNOW JESUS CHRIST

Deep down inside, humanity is crying for something—but they don't know what it is. The Bible even says, "For the creation was subjected to frustration, not by its own choice, but by the will of the one who subjected it" (Romans 8:20, NIV).

There is a gaping, empty place in your soul that can't be filled with a relationship . . . or with possessions . . . or with a position . . . or with education . . . or even with pleasure. It is an emptiness that only God can fill.

Keith Urban, a country music star, went into rehab some years ago for alcohol issues. He felt that taking that action had saved his marriage. In an interview he made this statement: "Playing massive stadiums isn't going to fill any hole in me."[3]

That was a wise statement. Urban is right. Even if you are a famous person in front of a stadium full of adoring people, there still will be that emptiness within you. In fact, it might even feel deeper because of that experience.

2. EVERYONE IS LONELY

You can even be in a crowd of people and be lonely. Albert Einstein, considered by many to be one of the most intelligent men who ever lived (and certainly one of the most famous) once said, "It is strange to be known so universally yet to be so lonely."

Brad Delp was the lead singer of the band Boston, a group that sold over twenty million albums. Boston was known for a number of songs, including, "More than a Feeling" and (ironically) "Peace of Mind."

But Brad Delp committed suicide in 2007. Clipped to his shirt was a suicide note in which he had written, "Mr. Brad Delp. *J'ai une ame solitaire.* I am a lonely soul."[4]

Maybe you would say, "Well, if I could just meet the right person, I will never be lonely again." But you can even be lonely when you are married. The problem is that we expect our spouses to fill a void in our lives that only God can fill.

Here is what it comes down to: your loneliness is a loneliness for God Himself.

3. EVERYONE FEELS GUILT

We all feel guilt from time to time and, by the way, that isn't always a bad thing. One of the reasons we feel guilt is because we are guilty! The Bible says that all are guilty. In Romans 3:23 we read, "For all have sinned and fall short of the glory of God."

You feel guilty because you have done wrong things. You feel guilty because you have broken God's commandments. You feel guilty because you have made unkind, selfish decisions. We have all felt that deep-down guilt in our lives.

I have good news for you. God can forgive you of your sin and remove that guilt from your life this very day—or night.

4. EVERYONE IS AFRAID TO DIE

The Bible speaks of those who are held in slavery by their fear of death. Steve Jobs, the CEO of Apple and one of the most brilliant people who ever lived, had to deal with severe health issues for years before his death in 2011. In an interview with *Fortune* magazine, he was quoted as saying, "Life is short, and we're all going to die really soon. It's true, you know."[5]

And it's true even if you are a genius, even if you are famous. Everyone has to come face-to-face with the fact that life is going to come to an end. Woody Allen said, "I'm not afraid of death. I just don't want to be there when it happens."

Sorry, Woody. You will be there.

But if you think death is an end of things, you're wrong. Death is the end of human existence, but then there is a life beyond. You have the choice of where you will experience that eternal life. There is a Heaven, in the presence of God, the angels, and many of your loved ones who have gone on before you. But there is also a life of eternal separation from God in a place called Hell.

We make that decision where we will spend eternity.

The Cure

So Naaman heard from the man of God about what he needed to do: "Go and wash in the Jordan seven times" (2 Kings 5:10).

He absolutely didn't want to do it. And I have an idea why.

I don't think he wanted to reveal his real condition to the watching eyes of the world. He wanted to hide his leprosy. I think he had covered it up expertly for quite a while with long garments and lots of armor. I would imagine that even some of his men weren't aware of his real condition. He would have to humble himself. He would have to get real with himself, with everyone else, and with God.

Finally one of his own guys essentially said, "Hey, General Naaman, with all due respect, why don't you give this thing a try? What have you got to lose?"

The general knew good counsel when he heard it. So he went down to the Jordan River, pulled off his breastplate, took off his helmet, and peeled off his shirt. In that moment, perhaps for the first time, his men saw the disfiguring effects of leprosy on his body. Some of them were no doubt shocked and amazed.

In our way, we all hide behind armor, don't we? We all have a façade that we live by and want others to believe. But the fact is that you are a hurting person who needs the touch of God. Peel off the armor and get honest and truthful with Him. Tell Him, "Lord, I need Your help."

That's what Naaman had to do. The proud military man disrobed, revealing his diseased body, waded into the Jordan River, and humbly immersed himself. When he came up again, he was the same Naaman.

He immersed himself again, with the same result. And again. How many times did the prophet tell him to go under water? Seven times. On the seventh dunk, don't you just imagine that he stayed in the water a little bit longer?

"Oh please, God of Israel, let it be true."

And it was. He came up out of the water with his leprosy gone. The Bible says that his skin was like that of a baby.

You know what a baby's skin is like. It's like silk. And that's how it was for Naaman. He was healed right there on the spot. Can you even imagine the joy that surged through him? He was healed! Clean! All of the worry and dread that had haunted him for who knows how long was gone in an instant.

Why This Story?

Someone might say, "Greg, why are you telling this story?"

Because it is a classic picture of a person without God—perhaps a person just like you. Like this famous Syrian general, you might have many of the elements the world says will bring happiness. But something is missing. Maybe you have wanted salvation, eternal life, and a relationship with God, but you have wanted those things on your own terms. You don't want to do it God's way.

Naaman didn't like God's terms one bit. In fact, he had come very close to blowing the whole thing off because it all seemed so humiliating to him. He had said, "I don't *want* to peel my armor off in front of people and dunk myself in the Jordan."

And you might say, "I want to have eternal life, but I don't want to admit that I'm a sinner and put my faith in Jesus Christ. I don't believe in organized religion."

Guess what? I don't believe in organized religion, either. Nor do I consider myself a religious person. To be frank, I have no interest whatsoever in religion. It doesn't draw me. It doesn't fascinate me. It doesn't appeal to me in the slightest degree. I have never been a religious person and never wanted to be a religious person.

But I *do* want to know God.

I *do* want to know the meaning of life.

I *do* want to fill the big hole in my heart.

And I *do* want to go to Heaven when I die—and I think you do, too.

It's Not on Our Terms

What the Bible tells us is that we can't come to God on our own terms. We can't make it up as we go along. We can't just walk up to a celestial, supernatural salad bar and say, "I'll take a little of this religion, a little of that religion, and then I will make up some of my own really weird stuff and throw it all together." What you end up with is a hodge-podge. What you end up with is nothing at all.

If you want to go to Heaven, you must come on God's terms. And that starts by admitting that you are a sinner.

Naaman had a choice: dunk and be healed, or don't dunk and die. You, in the same way, have a choice: Believe and be saved. Put your faith in Christ and live forever in Heaven, or don't believe and reject Him and face the repercussions.

To the person who feels empty, Jesus says, "I am the gate; whoever enters through me will be saved. . . . I have come that they may have life, and have it to the full" (John 10:9–10, NIV). In other words, Jesus is saying, "I will give you a dimension of life that is so full, you won't believe it."

To the person who feels lonely, Jesus says, "Look at me. I stand at the door. I knock. If you hear me call and open the door, I'll come right in and sit down to supper with you" (Revelation 3:20, MSG). You need never be lonely again! Jesus said, "Never will I leave you; never will I forsake you" (Hebrews 13:5, NIV).

To the person who feels guilt, the Bible says, "If we say that we have no sin, we deceive ourselves, and the truth is not in us. If we confess our sins, He is faithful and just to forgive us our sins and to cleanse us from all unrighteous-ness" (1 John 1:8–9). Our God has a big eraser, and He will use it in your life—*this very day, this very night*—if you will let Him remove your sin and your guilt.

For the person who is afraid to die, Jesus says, "I am the resurrection and the life. He who believes in Me, though he may die, he shall live. And whoever lives and believes in Me shall never die" (John 11:25–26). Death is not the end of our existence. If you put your faith in Jesus Christ, you will live forever in God's presence.

What do you need to do? Step one is to turn from your life of sin. Step one for General Naaman was to finally admit his need and acknowledge that he couldn't cure himself. In the same way, you have to admit your need and turn from your sin. The Bible says, "Repent therefore and be converted, that your sins may be blotted out, so that times of refreshing may come from the presence of the Lord" (Acts 3:19). And once again in the book of Acts we read, "God . . . now commands all men everywhere to repent" (17:30).

What does it meant to "repent"?

It's like hanging a U-turn on the road of life.

Not long ago I was riding my Harley out on a little road and came to a place where I had to turn around. I leaned into the turn and gave it a little gas because I didn't want my bike to fall over. Those big old hogs are heavy, and it's almost impossible for one guy to pick one up. So I made my U-turn carefully, and in a few seconds I was cruising in the opposite direction.

Repenting means doing a U-turn on the road of life. You stop walking away from God and start walking *toward* Him. When you do, something wonderful happens: *He comes to meet you!* In Psalm 79:8 the psalmist prayed, "May your mercy come quickly to meet us, for we are in desperate need" (NIV).

Stop going in the wrong direction, turn around, and start heading toward Christ. He will hurry to meet you.

SATISFACTION FOR THE SPIRITUALLY THIRSTY

Charlene McDaniel was one of the nine children of Charles and Stella McDaniel, who made their home in Friendship, Arkansas.

Charlene was strikingly beautiful. In fact, she was so pretty that people would tell her, "You look just like Marilyn Monroe."

Charles and Stella were Christians and took their children to church every Sunday, and Sunday nights as well. Charlene, however, didn't like church, didn't like what the Bible had to say, and didn't care at all for the so-called constraints of the Christian life. As soon as she was able, she rebelled against the rules of her Christian home and began to pursue a lifestyle of drinking and partying with friends. If anyone ever challenged what she was doing, she would bristle, completely rejecting their words.

She figured the best way to escape her parents' rules would be to get married. So when a handsome young guy came along and proposed to her, she accepted. That would be the first of seven, perhaps eight, marriages that she would find herself in as the years passed by.

She divorced this first husband shortly after she married him. They'd had a son together, her first of two. Then she married another man and became pregnant again and gave birth to a stillborn child. She was so disillusioned by that event that she went back to the party scene more than ever and decided that marriage wasn't for her.

As time went by, she had a fling with a guy whom she met in Long Beach and became pregnant again. Because it wasn't in vogue to have a baby out of wedlock in those days (as it is today with the Hollywood elite), she married another man and asked if he would put his name down on the birth certificate as the father of the child, which he agreed to do, and she had her second son.

They nicknamed this second son Pogo because he was mischievous like that cartoon character in the strips drawn by Walt Kelly years ago.

So Charlene McDaniel was a beautiful woman going from marriage to marriage, from divorce to divorce, on a quest looking for fulfillment, looking for meaning, looking for purpose in her life. Eventually, she sent Pogo to live with her parents for a few years. He also went to military school and lived with various aunts and uncles. Eventually Charlene realized that she couldn't keep passing off Pogo from family member to family member, so he lived with her for a time.

It was a pretty frightening time for this young boy to see his mom come home at four in the morning after a night of drinking. It was stressful to see her in abusive relationship after abusive relationship. On one occasion, one of Charlene's lovers almost killed her, hitting her across the head and leaving her for dead. Pogo climbed out of his bedroom window to call the police and an ambulance.

Charlene continued her lifestyle, her empty quest for meaning in life, with circumstances sliding from bad to worse.

But something unexpected happened to Pogo . . . or I should say me.

An Unexpected Conversion

Charlene was my mom. And when I gave my life to Jesus Christ at the age of seventeen, I longed for her to come to faith as well. But she rebelled against my influence just as she had rejected the influence of her parents as they raised her in the church.

As I became a pastor and evangelist, I knew that she was proud of me and of my accomplishments. But she didn't want to make a commitment to Christ herself and would clam up whenever the subject arose. She still had her beauty, and she still drew men.

But one day when she was under the influence, she got into a head-on collision with a car on Jamboree Road in Newport Beach, California, and it almost killed her. It also disfigured her once-beautiful face. In addition to this, the lifestyle she had chosen was taking its toll on her health.

She was still resistant to the gospel, but we were beginning to see some hopeful signs. She was just beginning to soften a little bit. For instance, we would go out for a meal, and I would always pray before the meal, whether I was with believers or nonbelievers. She began to like those prayers and even wait for them. After a while, I realized that she wouldn't eat her food until we prayed. And if I forgot to pray, she reminded me. That was a hopeful sign.

She would come to our evangelistic crusades, but I never saw her make that commitment.

She always said, "I don't want to talk about it."

The years went by, and she said it over and over again: "Greg, I just don't want to talk about it."

All of those years of drinking, smoking, and partying finally began to take a toll on her, and her body was giving out. She experienced some kidney failure and had to be on dialysis every week.

One day I felt really impressed by the Lord to go over to her house and have that conversation about her soul.

I said to my wife, "I feel really led by God."

She said, "Go do it."

So I went over to my mother's house and said, "Mom, I need to talk to you."

We sat down at the kitchen table.

I said, "I want to talk to you about your soul.".

"I don't want to talk about it," she said.

"Mom," I replied, "today we *are* going to talk about it."

I'm so glad we had that conversation because it resulted in her making a recommitment to Jesus Christ.

And one month later, she passed into eternity. I know she is in Heaven right now and that I will see her again.

It wasn't easy for my mother and me to finally have that all-important conversation about eternity. But in many ways, it was the best conversation we ever had.

It was a glorious thing that my mother came back to the faith she had left as a teenager. But it also was sad that she had spent most of her years looking for a man, a marriage, and a relationship to fill the great void in her heart. And it never worked.

A Biblical Parallel

Why do I bring up my mother's story?

Because it so closely parallels the story told by the apostle John in the fourth chapter of his gospel. This is the story of a very empty woman, a woman who thought that romance and sex would fill the empty places in her life. Like my mother Charlene, this was a woman who went from husband to husband, hoping to find her prince. Apparently, after her fifth husband, she just gave up.

The woman in John 4 had been used and abused and disillusioned. We can assume that this woman, whom we know as the woman at the well, had once been beautiful—perhaps strikingly so. But we can well imagine that at this point in her life, after five husbands, her beauty was beginning to fade. The husbands were gone, and friends of days gone by had abandoned her. She was living with a man to whom she seemed indifferent. She basically was a woman alone—until she had an encounter with Jesus Christ, and her life was turned around.

In this story we not only see how the spiritual thirst of a person can be satisfied, but we also see how to effectively reach a person who is searching.

Meeting at a Well

So [Jesus] left Judea and returned to Galilee.

He had to go through Samaria on the way. Eventually he came to the Samaritan village of Sychar, near the field that Jacob gave to his son Joseph. Jacob's well was there; and Jesus, tired from the long walk, sat wearily beside the well about noontime. Soon a Samaritan woman came to draw water, and Jesus said to her, "Please give me a drink." He was alone at the time because his disciples had gone into the village to buy some food.

The woman was surprised, for Jews refuse to have anything to do with Samaritans. She said to Jesus, "You are a Jew, and I am a Samaritan woman. Why are you asking me for a drink?"

Jesus replied, "If you only knew the gift God has for you and who you are speaking to, you would ask me, and I would give you living water."

"But sir, you don't have a rope or a bucket," she said, "and this well is very deep. Where would you get this living water? And besides, do you think you're greater than our ancestor Jacob, who gave us this well? How can you offer better water than he and his sons and his animals enjoyed?"

Jesus replied, "Anyone who drinks this water will soon become thirsty again. But those who drink the water I give will never be thirsty again. It becomes a fresh, bubbling spring within them, giving them eternal life."

"Please, sir," the woman said, "give me this water! Then I'll never be thirsty again, and I won't have to come here to get water."

"Go and get your husband," Jesus told her.

"I don't have a husband," the woman replied.

Jesus said, "You're right! You don't have a husband—for you have had five husbands, and you aren't even married to the man you're living with now. You certainly spoke the truth!"

"Sir," the woman said, "you must be a prophet." (John 4:3–19, NLT)

At the beginning of this account, the Bible tells us that "He had to go through Samaria on the way." Under normal circumstances, *no* orthodox Jew would *ever* go to Galilee through Samaria. In fact, he would go miles and miles out of his way to avoid Samaria altogether. Most of the Jews of Jesus' time who wanted to travel from Judea to Galilee would take the long way around. This would make for a journey of about five days, even though there was a direct route that passed through Samaria that would take half the time.

Why would they do that?

One simple answer: prejudice.

The Jews wanted nothing to do with the Samaritans, and the feeling was mutual. They hated one another—not unlike the passionate conflict between Israelis and Palestinians to this very day. Yet we read in this story that Jesus *had* to go.

Jesus, a good Jew, *had* to go through Samaria? Why?

Was it because He wanted to take the shortcut and save some time?

No. He had to go through Samaria because there was a miserably unhappy, burned-out woman who was on a search for meaning in life. And unbeknownst to her, she had an appointment with God on that particular day.

The Lord and His Detour: What Does This Teach Us?

What can we learn from the deliberate detour that Jesus took through Samaria?

PRINCIPLE 1: WE NEED TO REACH OUT TO PEOPLE WHO AREN'T NECESSARILY LIKE US

The conventional wisdom for sharing my faith might go something like this: I need to find someone who looks and maybe thinks just like me and then go talk to him or her because I can relate to that person. (So therefore, by that logic, I'm only going to speak to really handsome bald men.) In other words, for the most part I'm going to avoid approaching someone who is a little different from me because we might not relate to one another.

Obviously there is some validity to that. But it can also put you in a position of limiting God.

I believe in the power of the Word of God to cross *every* barrier.

There is a trend in churches today where leadership actually will custom design their ministry to fit a certain demographic. For instance, some might say, "We want to have an affluent suburban church. Therefore, this is our target audience, and we'll develop programs, our style of music, and everything else to reach this target audience in hopes they will come."

Another group might say, "We want to reach bikers. That is our demographic."

Others see themselves as a surfer church or a cowboy church. The list goes on.

I believe the church should reach *all* of those people—and reach them in the same congregation—bikers next to surfers, African Americans next to Caucasians, Asians next to Hispanics, all of us worshiping together and setting aside our differences because we are brothers and sisters in Christ and part of God's family.

To me, the beauty and genius of the church that Jesus started is that when a nonbeliever walks in, he or she doesn't see a bunch of people who are the same age, the same race, and of the same socioeconomic background. Instead, he or she will see people who are different from one another and yet have become one because of their faith in the Lord.

In Galatians 3:28 we read, "We are no longer Jews or Greeks or slaves or free men or even merely men or women, but we are all the same—we are Christians; we are one in Christ Jesus" (TLB).

I remember standing at the back of our church some time ago, talking to a guy who seemed to be an obvious "biker dude," dressed in all the biker leather and gear.

He introduced me to a sweet elderly lady. Smiling, he said, "We just led her to the Lord the other day."

As I looked at the rough-looking biker and the petite senior citizen, I was having a little trouble processing the situation.

I said, "How on earth would you ever even meet each other?"

"It was after our Easter service," he said. He and his biker buddy had been in a Jack in the Box restaurant getting a meal when they decided to go over and talk to this eighty-year-old lady, Bonnie, and her ninety-two-year-old husband, Tippy. The bikers invited the couple to church, they came, and both of them made a commitment to Christ. Now they have been the best of friends and have been walking with the Lord together for more than two years.

These men were willing to cross a barrier, just as Jesus was willing to cross a barrier.

Jesus met this Samaritan woman at noon, by the town well. Most of the women would have come to the well earlier in the day, before the sun got hot, to exchange the latest gossip and draw some water. But she came alone, in the heat of the day, because she was a social outcast. She had been ostracized, and she had no friends.

It must have been quite surprising for her to come to the well and see a visitor—someone she didn't recognize. And not only that, but He clearly was a *Jew*, a rabbi! She could tell these things by the way He dressed. A rabbi had a thin strip of blue at the bottom of His robe, and it may have been that Jesus had that strip too.

As a result of what she saw at the well, this Samaritan woman undoubtedly braced herself for a confrontation—or at the very least, a hateful sneer and stony silence.

Can you imagine her surprise when this rabbi gently spoke to her and asked her for something to drink? He was deliberately engaging her, and He had to cross a huge barrier to do even that.

PRINCIPLE 2: WE HAVE TO GO WHERE PEOPLE ARE

Jesus went to Samaria, into this woman's world, to reach her on that level. And that is what we need to do. We want to go to where people are living and walking and functioning and then invade that place with the gospel message.

PRINCIPLE 3: WE NEED TO CARE ABOUT THE PEOPLE THAT WE SPEAK TO

Again, John 4:4 says, "He needed to go through Samaria." Why did He have to go? Because He had a burden for this lost woman.

PRINCIPLE 4: WE NEED TO KEEP AT IT, EVEN WHEN WE ARE TIRED

John 4:6 tells us that "Jesus, tired from the long walk, sat wearily beside the well about noontime" (NLT).

What a picture! There was God in human form, exhausted, wiped out! You know the feeling, don't you? It's like those times when you have said, "I can't go another step farther. I've got to sit down for a minute and rest."

The disciples had basically said, "Lord, we're going into town to get some food. Do you want to come?"

And Jesus would have replied, "No guys, you go on ahead. I'll just sit here by this well for a while."

If I had been God in that moment, it would have been a huge temptation for me to simply speak that food into existence. Waiting for food is always hard for me. I'll order something in a restaurant and want to eat it right away. I will say, "When is the food coming?"

When my wife is cooking a meal, I'll walk into the kitchen and say, "When will it be done?"

If I had been as weary and hungry as Jesus was surely weary and hungry, I would have spoken an In-N-Out burger into existence. So what if it hadn't been invented yet? God knows all things and could have done whatever He wanted.

But Jesus never used His miraculous powers for His own benefit. That is what the Devil tempted Him to do during the temptation in the wilderness. After Jesus had been fasting for forty days, the Evil One essentially said to Him, "Hey, why don't You take this rock and turn it into a nice, fresh piece of bread if you're so hungry?"

But Jesus refused that temptation.

When John wrote that Jesus was tired from the journey, we can be sure that He was really exhausted. When you read the Gospels, you realize that Jesus hardly ever had a moment to Himself. It wasn't only the physical strain of all that walking, those meager meals, and sleeping on the ground. He must have also had to deal with a tremendous spiritual and emotional drain. That's why He would spend long nights in prayer to prepare Himself for everything the next day would hold.

We have all kinds of advisers and counselors these days warning us about burning ourselves out with too much busyness. And yes, there is some truth in what they say.

But at the same time, there is nothing wrong with getting tired in the service of the Lord. I've been a pastor for more than forty years, and I will tell you that I have been tired. I have been tired *in* ministry but never tired *of* ministry. What greater thing could I ever do than serve the Lord?

There are many worse things you could be tired from. You could be tired from partying all night and not getting your rest. You could be tired from covering up your sins or escaping your own lies. You could be tired from running around in a frenzy, trying to have fun.

I'd rather be tired in the Lord's work. I'd rather be tired from a long prayer meeting. I'd rather be tired from counseling a troubled soul. I'd rather be tired from helping people with a need.

People might say, "Hey, man, take it easy." But where does it say that in the Scriptures? I'll tell you where! That's what a man who had no time for God said to himself after building bigger buildings to house all of his possessions. Jesus told the story in Luke 12:

> "A rich man had a fertile farm that produced fine crops. He said to himself, 'What should I do? I don't have room for all my crops.' Then he said, 'I know! I'll tear down my barns and build bigger ones. Then I'll have room enough to store all my wheat and other goods. And I'll sit back and say to myself, "'My friend, you have enough stored away for years to come. Now take it easy! Eat, drink, and be merry!'"
>
> "But God said to him, 'You fool! You will die this very night. Then who will get everything you worked for?' " (verses 16–21, NLT)

The Bible tells us that we are to press on, to not be weary in well-doing, and to run the race. In the book of Romans, Paul wrote, "Let us not allow slackness to spoil our work and let us keep the fires of the spirit burning, as we do our work for God" (12:11, PH). Our greatest recreation and rest will come later when we are in Heaven.

Oswald Sanders once said that the world is run by tired men. And I think you will find that effective ministries are run by tired pastors, and effective outreaches are run by tired, weary Christians.

In 1 Thessalonians 2:9 Paul said, "Don't you remember, dear brothers and sisters, how hard we worked among you? Night and day we toiled to earn a living so that we would not be a burden to any of you as we preached God's Good News to you" (NLT).

PRINCIPLE 5: WE MUST SHARE THE TRUTH OF GOD WITH TACT AND LOVE

Notice how Jesus made conversation with this woman and bridged the great gap that had been between them.

"Please give me a drink" (John 4:7, NLT).

"You are a Jew, and I am a Samaritan woman. Why are you asking me for a drink?" (verse 9, NLT).

"If you only knew the gift God has for you and who you are speaking to, you would ask me, and I would give you living water" (verse 10, NLT).

"Where would you get this living water? And besides, do you think you're greater than our ancestor Jacob, who gave us this well? How can you offer better water than he and his sons and his animals enjoyed?" (verses 11–12, NLT).

It was a *dialogue*. He wasn't lecturing her; He was engaging her. He had piqued her curiosity and arrested her attention. He spoke, and He listened.

Often when we share our faith, it's more like a monologue: *I'm going to preach a sermon to you, so shut up and listen, and I won't let you get a word in edgewise.*

That is not effective communication. Learn to listen. Ask questions. Pay attention to what other people are saying, and respond appropriately. Show how the Word of God has everything that they need in life. Ask them questions that get them to think about their lives.

That is what Jesus was doing. He was appealing to her inner spiritual thirst.

In verse 10 He threw out the bait: "If you only knew the gift God has for you and who you are speaking to, you would ask me, and I would give you living water" (NLT).

Initially her response was sarcastic and flippant—perhaps even cynical. She was verbally jousting with this stranger—possibly because of her general attitude toward men: *Men are all the same. They're all dogs. Corrupt. Selfish. They don't care. So who is this guy? What's his angle?*

As she continued to converse with Jesus, however, she knew in her heart that something made Him different. She could see that He cared.

In the course of their brief dialogue, Jesus gave this woman three important facts. He told her who He was, what He had to offer, and how she could receive it.

Jesus Gave Her Three Facts

1. HE TOLD HER WHO HE WAS

In verse 12, the Samaritan woman asked, "Are You greater than our [ancestor] Jacob?" This is almost humorous to me. Jesus could have said, "Jacob? *Jacob?* Let me tell you a little bit about Jacob. I know him pretty well. Remember the incident described in Genesis 32 when Jacob wrestled all night with a mysterious stranger? When it was all over, Jacob named the place Peniel, because he said, 'For I have seen God face to face.' Listen to Me. I was the One who wrestled with Jacob that night. And do you know what else? I whipped him."

He could have said that, but He didn't. He let the Jacob comment go right on by. She wasn't ready for that kind of information right then, so He didn't share it with her. It was too much.

When we share the gospel with someone, we need to remember to keep it simple and to avoid rabbit trails. We also need to bear in mind that a non-Christian won't understand everything about the truth of the gospel.

One of the things I have so admired about Billy Graham's preaching through the years is his laser-beam simplicity with the essential gospel message. There are certain elements that must be there in any gospel message, and many other side trips that need to be left out.

My objective is not to sway someone to my political views. My objective is not to move someone toward my worldview, at least initially. What I want to do before any-thing else is to help them move toward God to have their sins forgiven—regardless of their lifestyle, regardless of what they've been involved in up to that point. Then, once they have met Christ and begin to study the Bible, I believe that the Lord Himself will begin to change their outlook and habits of life.

Sometimes in the church we get the cart before the horse. We are almost proclaiming political viewpoints or contemporary moral issues before Christ Himself.

I want people to hear the gospel and come to faith in Jesus. That is what the Lord was doing.

At one point in the conversation, the Samaritan woman tried to get Jesus off on a rabbit trail regarding the right place to worship God. "We think it's in Samaria," she was telling Him, "but you Jews claim it's in Jerusalem."

Jesus brought her right back on message, telling her that whoever worships God must worship Him "in spirit and truth" (verse 23). That returned the conversation to the essential message He had been giving her: *I will satisfy your deepest spiritual thirst.*

This was a woman who had been going in and out of marriages, which isn't uncommon in our times, either. Someone will have an initial euphoria upon meeting someone else and will imagine they are "in love." They will call it "falling in love" or maybe "love at first sight."

"Oh, I have butterflies in my stomach. My mouth goes dry and my mind goes blank. I don't know what to say. I'm just so excited when I'm near her (or him). My heart is just aflutter."

If you end up marrying that person, do you really want to repeat that experience every single day? I have been married to my wife for more than forty years, and I can truthfully say that I love her now more than the day I married her. But I don't want to have those initial experiences rerun every single day. If I came down the stairs and said, "Cathe, my mouth has gotten dry and my mind is blank and my heart is aflutter," she would think that I was having a heart attack and call 911.

Genuine love has to deepen and grow through the years. You understand that you have made a commitment, you have given your vows to that person for better or for worse, for richer or for poorer, in sickness and in health.

So many people say such words at their wedding and then quickly abandon those promises when they encounter difficult times. Someone has said, "What's so remarkable about love at first sight? It's when people have been looking at each other for years that it becomes remarkable!"

I love the definition of married love that C. S. Lewis gave:

> Love . . . is not merely a feeling. It is a deep unity, maintained by the will and deliberately strengthened by habit; reinforced by the grace which both partners ask, and receive from God. . . . "Being in love" first moved them to promise fidelity: this quieter love enables them to keep the promise. It is on this love that the engine of marriage is run: being in love was the explosion that started it.[1]

Real love requires real commitment, but for whatever reason, the Samaritan woman wouldn't keep that commitment. As soon as the initial euphoria and excitement of a new relationship wore off, she was off to a new conquest, off to a new guy. The years went by, and the men in her life used her and abused her—including the one she was currently living with.

Jesus said to her, "If you will drink of this well you will thirst again."

When He made that statement, He knew that the same thing could be said over all the "wells" in her life.

It's true for you and me as well. You could write it over the well of success. You could write it over the well of possessions. You could certainly write it over the well of pleasure. *If you drink of this water, you will thirst again.* You always want what you haven't got.

2. HE TOLD HER WHAT HE HAD TO OFFER

Of the many unsuccessful diets I cycle through, now and then I will try the Atkins diet, where you're allowed plenty of proteins and fat but have to avoid carbohydrates. My problem is that I go on the diet . . . for a while. Then I weaken and go off it. My wife actually has said to me, "I think you're on a weight-gain diet right now, because you eat all of the fattening stuff on Atkins, and then you go and eat carbs."

It is possible to lose weight on this diet. I have lost pounds—but then gained them right back, over and over. The first day on the diet is amazing. I can eat a cheese omelet with bacon on the side. I can actually have two chicken breasts for dinner and munch on cheese in between meals. Best of all, instead of using milk in a latte, you are supposed to use cream!

But after three or four days on the diet, I start dreaming of carbs. I will say to my wife, "I dreamed about pizza last night." I remember telling her at one point, "I have an emptiness in my life that only carbs can fill!"

After another couple of days, I don't care about bacon. I don't want any more cheese. I don't want any more meat. And I don't care about lattes made with cream. I want *bread.* I want French fries. I want cereal. I want pancakes.

That's a poor illustration, perhaps, of someone who has excluded God from his or her life. No matter what that individual might say or insist about themselves, they have a craving for God—a deep inner longing for their Creator.

In Isaiah 26:9, the prophet cries out to the Lord, "My soul yearns for you in the night; in the morning my spirit longs for you" (NIV).

That's how it was for this Samaritan woman, and Jesus knew it immediately. So He began telling her what she needed to do to quench that deep inner thirst.

In John 4:14, He spoke of what He has to offer, saying, "Whoever drinks of the water that I shall give . . ." What did He mean by "living water"? He was basically describing water that moved—like a stream or river—as opposed to water that was stagnant.

3. HE TOLD HER HOW TO GET IT

Jesus had been speaking to her of something more than physical water, and she knew it. But she was still playing coy with Him and said, "Please, sir, . . . give me this water! Then I'll never be thirsty again, and I won't have to come here to get water" (John 4:15, NLT).

From that point on, the conversation took a more direct turn:

"Go and get your husband," Jesus told her.

"I don't have a husband," the woman replied.

(verses 16–17, NLT)

And He essentially answered, "That's right, girl. You don't have a husband. You've been married and divorced five times, and now you're living with a guy."

I can imagine her mouth dropping open at that point. That woke her up.

Why did Jesus make that statement? Because she had been playing little games with Him, and it was time for her to take the conversation seriously.

He was saying, in essence, "I know what's going on with you. And before you can drink of the living water, before you can get right with Me, this sin needs to be identified and repented of."

This reminds us of the essential fact that there can be no conversion without conviction and repentance.

Some people want to bring Jesus in as a wonderful additive to life. They say to themselves, "I'll keep living the way that I have been living and do what I want to do, but I'll add Jesus to the mix, and everything will be great."

No, it won't.

Not knowing how else to reply, the woman said to Jesus, "Sir, . . . you must be a prophet" (verse 19, NLT). And of course, He was and is far more than a prophet; He is the very Son of God.

With the truth beginning to dawn on her, she said cautiously, "I know the Messiah is coming—the one who is called Christ. When he comes, he will explain everything to us" (verse 25, NLT).

That's when Jesus dropped the bombshell: "I AM the Messiah!" (verse 26, NLT).

Boom! The Samaritan woman believed right on the spot. And in that moment, she became the first female evangelist in the New Testament. The biblical account says, "The woman left her water jar beside the well and ran back to the village, telling everyone, 'Come and see a man who told me everything I ever did! Could he possibly be the Messiah?' So the people came streaming from the village to see him" (verses 28–30, NLT).

Even though her newfound faith was only moments old, she just had to tell others.

A Final Question

Coming back to where I began this message, with the story of my mother, it's clear to me now that for many years she had been trying to satisfy a spiritual thirst with something or someone other than Jesus Christ.

She had been raised in the church and, deep down, she knew what was true. And what she discovered very late in the game was that what she had been searching for her whole life was very near at hand. She was like the prodigal son in Jesus' story. He realized that everything he had been searching for in life was right there in his father's house.

Have you discovered that yet?

Nothing this world has to offer will satisfy your deepest spiritual thirst.

If you drink at the well of possessions, you will thirst again. Jesus said, "What will it profit a man if he gains the whole world, and loses his own soul?" (Mark 8:36).

If you drink at the well of pleasure, you will thirst again. The Bible says that sin may be pleasurable for a season (see Hebrews 11:25, KJV), but it also flatly declares that "the wages of sin is death" (Romans 6:23).

You can drink at the well of what seems to be "the perfect relationship." But the woman in this story undoubtedly had high hopes, too. Yet she went from marriage to marriage, from divorce to divorce. Only God can fill that void.

The Samaritan woman had run back into town, telling everyone she met, "Come, see a Man who told me all things that I ever did" (John 4:29).

Jesus offers the same invitation. He says, "Come and see. Come and see who I am for yourself."

8 Chapter

THE PURSUIT
OF HAPPINESS

I heard a story about an older man who was talking to a young law student about his future plans.

"All right, son," he said, "tell me what you want to do with your life after you graduate from law school."

"Well," the student replied, "I'd like to get a job and start making some money."

The older man nodded. "That's good," he said. "Then what?"

"I would like to get married," came the reply.

"That's good too," the older man said. "Then what?"

"A family," the student said. "I want to start a family."

"Okay. Then what?"

"Well, I'd want to raise my kids and . . . put them in good schools."

"That sounds good. Then what?"

"I hope that I'll make enough money to eventually slow down—and maybe get a second home, even."

"Great," the older man said. "Then what?"

The young man had probably never thought so far

ahead in his life, but he replied, "I would imagine I'll go into retirement. If my health is still good, my wife and I will be able travel and see something of the world."

"Right," his elder nodded appreciatively. "Then what?"

"Well, I guess then I will die."

The older man said, "Right. That's good. *Then what?*"

Then what? Eternity.

There are at least two things that are true about every person on this planet: we all want to be happy, and, unless Jesus comes back first, we're all going to die. The statistics on death are very impressive: one out of every one person will die. No one can change that.

I remember glancing at the cover of a *Time* magazine in an airport and seeing this headline: "Can Google Solve Death?"

Are you ready for the answer?

No. They can't.

The article apparently detailed Google's venture to extend the human lifespan.[1] That's fine, I guess. They could be involved in even less productive things. But Jesus said, "I am the living one. I died, but look—I am alive forever and ever! And I hold the keys of death and the grave" (Revelation 1:18, NLT).

The keys of life and death are in the hands of Jesus Christ, and there is no getting around that.

Big Questions

Every thinking person gets around to asking those big questions in life.

Why am I here?

What is the meaning of life?

What will happen to me when I die?

Maybe you've asked such questions as well.

I heard a story about a drunk guy who was down on his hands and knees under a streetlight, clearly looking for something. A police officer approached him and said, "Sir, did you lose something?"

"Yes!" he said. "I've lost my wallet."

"You lost it here, then?" asked the officer.

"No, no, no," the inebriated man replied, "I lost it across the street."

"Then why aren't you looking over there instead of here?"

"Because there's no light *over there*," he explained.

In the same way, you might be on a search for truth. That's good. But you won't be very successful in your search if you are looking in the wrong place. Some people search throughout their entire lives and never find what they're looking for. That's tragic, because the answers are as near as your Bible. Jesus Christ Himself has those answers.

The Pursuit of Happiness

In our nation's founding document, the Declaration of Independence, our nation's framers wrote these words: "We hold these Truths to be self-evident, that all Men are created equal, that they are endowed, by their CREATOR, with certain unalienable Rights, that among these are Life, Liberty, and the Pursuit of Happiness."

The pursuit of happiness? How's that going for us as a nation?

More to the point, how's that going for *you*? Are you a happy person?

Some time ago, *Forbes* magazine devoted its seventy-fifth anniversary issue to a single topic: Why do we feel so bad when we have it so good?[2]

At the age of thirty-two, comedian Dave Chappelle certainly had realized his dreams. The ink on the contract was hardly dry when Chappelle mysteriously disappeared and surfaced eight thousand miles away, in South Africa. Chappelle literally walked away from the third season of his television show. Why did he do it? Why did he walk away from all that money? He was quoted as saying, "The higher up I go, for some reason, the less happy I am."[3]

I read an article about a couple in Brooklyn who had a call-in radio show called *The Pursuit of Happiness.* This married couple would offer callers advice on how to lead happier lives, telling them to think positively and trust their intuition. But apparently they were the ones who needed help because they both committed suicide.[4]

Where is happiness to be found?

Let me begin by telling you where it is *not* found.

1. BEING BEAUTIFUL OR HANDSOME WON'T BRING PERSONAL HAPPINESS

You see people today trying to create the perfect body through cosmetic surgery. I read that 94 percent of girls aged eighteen and under wish they were more beautiful.

Eighty-five percent of women over forty say they are not as attractive as the average woman. That is probably why last year, Americans spent an estimated $11.4 billion on cosmetic surgery fees—and probably $4 billion more when you factor in facility fees and anesthesia.

Why?

Because they want to reach some kind of perfect state; they want to look like the people they see in the magazines. The truth is, of course, that the people in the magazines don't even look like the people in the magazines. They've been Photoshopped! Others pump their faces so full of Botox that they can't even show expression anymore. They will say, "I'm really happy right now, but I can't move my face."

Maybe you think that life would be better if you acquired a bunch of tattoos. I won't comment much on this except to warn you that the cute little Tweety Bird of today might become Big Bird tomorrow if you get larger. That sweet little butterfly might turn into a scary pterodactyl.

2. HAVING POSSESSIONS WON'T BRING PERSONAL HAPPINESS

There was a recent *Time* magazine article with the headline, "Money: The Real Truth about Money." In the article the writer made this statement: "Clinical depression is 3 to 10 times as common today than two generations ago. . . . Money jangles in our wallets and purses like never before, but we are basically no happier for it, and for many, more money leads to depression."[5]

In fact, the Bible told us this very thing a long time ago. In the book of Proverbs we read, "Just as Death and Destruction are never satisfied, so human desire is never satisfied" (Proverbs 27:20, NLT).

Author Jack Higgins is one of the most successful writers on earth. His thriller novels have sold more than 250 million copies in 60 languages. When asked by a magazine interviewer what he knew now that he wished he had known earlier in life, the accomplished author responded, "That when you get to the top, there's nothing there."[6]

Years ago, King Solomon, who in his day was the wealthiest man around, penned these words:

All things are wearisome,
> more than one can say.
The eye never has enough of seeing,
> nor the ear its fill of hearing.
What has been will be again,
> what has been done will be done again;
> there is nothing new under the sun.
(Ecclesiastes 1:8–9, NIV)

Material things will not make you happy. If you have the money, you can push the envelope and get the latest smartphone, gadgets, sound systems, or the biggest flat-panel screen to hang on your wall. I think the biggest one out now is 152 inches. You have to sit two neighborhoods away to watch it!

None of these things will make you happy. The glow will begin to wear off before you have your Visa card back in your pocket.

Even relationships won't bring lasting happiness. Inevitably, parents will disappoint children. Children will disappoint parents. Husbands will disappoint wives, and wives will disappoint husbands. Boyfriends and girlfriends will continually disappoint each other.

Hugh Hefner, creator of the *Playboy* empire, has all of the money, power, and women any man could want. But he has said, "My life has been a quest for a world where the words to the songs are true."[7]

Can you hear the emptiness in those words?

3. PURSUING PLEASURE AND FAME WON'T BRING PERSONAL HAPPINESS

If you live for pleasure, you will never find it. The Bible says, "But she who lives in pleasure is dead while she lives" (1 Timothy 5:6).

Someone might say, "But if I were famous, if everyone knew my name, I'm sure I would be happy."

Probably not.

Johnny Depp is one of the most successful actors living today, and one of the few stars whose films have grossed $7.6 billion worldwide.[8] In an interview he said that thoughts of retirement pop up "every day," and he spoke of that certain point where he imagines that he'll "just take it down to the bare minimum and concentrate on, I guess, living life. Really living life. And going some-where where you don't have to be on the run, or sneak in through the kitchen. . . . When you get old enough or get a few brain cells back, you realize that, on some level, you lived the life of a fugitive."[9]

It's so ironic. Many of the people who are admired and envied by so many are overcome with the emptiness of their lives. When will we get the wake-up call that we can't find happiness without God?

It's a basic fact of human existence: if there is no God, there is no happiness. But if you know God, you have the opportunity for lasting happiness—and something even more than happiness, even more than personal peace. If you put your faith in Jesus Christ, you can have the hope that you will go to Heaven when you die.

There is nothing, nothing, nothing more important than that.

You realize that as you get older. When you are young, you don't think so much about the afterlife. But as the years go by, you think about it more and more—especially when you have someone close to you go there before you.

As I mentioned earlier, our son went to be with the Lord in 2008. It was the hardest day of our lives and something we still cry about. We miss him deeply. However, because we have put our faith in Jesus Christ, and because our son had put his faith in Christ, we know there will be a great heav-enly reunion one day. That is the great hope of every man or woman who has put faith in Jesus Christ.

But here is the caution: you can even be raised in the church and know all about God without really knowing Him in a personal relationship. That was the case for a young man we read about in the gospel of Matthew.

A Man with an Empty Place

The gospel writer tells the story of a rich and powerful young man who had everything going his way in life. From what we see in the account, he seemed to be a moral guy, devout and sincere. Even so, there was something missing in his life. Apparently he had been hearing a lot about this unusual rabbi from Galilee, and he wanted to see the Teacher for himself.

Finally the day came when he got that opportunity. He had an appointment with the Son of God—and the Creator of the Universe.

Someone came to Jesus with this question:

"Teacher, what good deed must I do to have eternal life?"

"Why ask me about what is good?" Jesus replied. "There is only One who is good. But to answer your question—if you want to receive eternal life, keep the commandments."

"Which ones?" the man asked.

And Jesus replied: "'You must not murder. You must not commit adultery. You must not steal. You must not testify falsely. Honor your father and mother. Love your neighbor as yourself.'"

"I've obeyed all these commandments," the young man replied. "What else must I do?"

Jesus told him, "If you want to be perfect, go and sell all your possessions and give the money to the poor, and you will have treasure in heaven. Then come, follow me."

But when the young man heard this, he went away sad, for he had many possessions.

(Matthew 19:16–22, NLT)

This New Testament portrait of a wealthy young man also could be a picture of people whom you know right now. In fact, it might be a picture of yourself.

Luke's version of the account calls him a "ruler" (see Luke 18:18). To be a Jewish ruler at this time, you had to be at least thirty. In today's terms, we might say that this young man climbed his corporate ladder quickly. No doubt he wore the latest fashions and drove the coolest chariot in town.

But there was something missing in his life, and he knew it.

When Jesus quoted some biblical commandments to him, he replied that he'd kept them all.

Sometimes I will hear people say, "I live by the Ten Commandments. That's all the religion I need."

I will say, "Really? Can you *name* the Ten Commandments?"

"No," they will reply, "but I live by them."

Not long ago, I read a survey revealing that more participants knew the names of the four Beatles than could recall even one command from the Ten Commandments.

Why did Jesus quote several of the Ten Commandments to this young man? He quoted them because He knew that no one can keep the Ten Commandments. Every one of us has broken the commandments. You may have even broken all of the commandments.

Have you ever murdered anyone? Even if you have, God would forgive you if you have repented of your sin.

There is a man in the Bible who was hunting down Christians. He hated all followers of Jesus. Ironically, he thought he was doing the work of God. His name was Saul. He came from Tarsus. One day that wicked man encountered none other than the risen Lord on the road to Damascus. Jesus said, "Saul, Saul, why are you persecuting Me?" (Acts 9:4). That man, guilty of murder, turned from his sin and was forgiven. He became the great apostle Paul. God can change you and forgive you no matter what you have done.

You might say, "I have never murdered anyone. I would never do that." But Jesus told us in His Sermon on the Mount that hating and despising someone in your heart can be just like murdering them. Have you ever hated someone so much that you wanted to kill them? Let me restate the question: Have you ever driven on the freeway? Let's be honest. We have broken that commandment.

Jesus also told the young man, "You must not commit adultery." What does that even mean?

Adultery is having sex with someone other than your wife or husband if you are married, and *fornication*, another biblical word, is having sex before you are married. Both of these acts are sins before God. The Bible says in Hebrews 13:4, "Marriage should be honored by all, and the marriage bed kept pure, for God will judge the adulterer and all the sexually immoral" (NIV).

Again, however, in the Sermon on the Mount, Jesus took this commandment a step further. He said, "You have heard the commandment that says, 'You must not commit adultery.' But I say, anyone who even looks at a woman with lust has already committed adultery with her in his heart" (Matthew 5:27–28, NLT).

We have all broken these commandments. We have all crossed the line. We have all sinned.

Jesus probably quoted the commandments to this young man so that he would wake up and realize that he had fallen short—and that he needed a Savior. But the man who knelt before Jesus that day thought he had walked in perfection. He told the Lord that he had obeyed all these commandments.

Another gospel tells us that at this point, "Jesus looked at him and loved him" (Mark 10:21, NIV).

Actually, the account would have made more sense to me if it read, "Jesus looked at him and smacked him alongside the head." What was this guy talking about? There's no way that he kept all those commandments from boyhood on.

Even so, Jesus looked at this brash, arrogant young man and—despite his sinfulness and pride—loved him.

I find that very encouraging.

No matter who you are or what you've done—even if you've been walking around with a prideful attitude—God loves you. But that doesn't mean He wants to leave you the way you are. He wants to change you. After you have turned from your sin and called out to Him for salvation, He will at first forgive you and then help you get started on a new life.

Jesus was quoting the commandments to this young man so that he could see that he fell short of the glory of God. As it says in the book of James, "For whoever keeps the whole law and yet stumbles at just one point is guilty of breaking all of it" (2:10, NIV).

Every one of us has broken multiple commandments of God. But even if you had somehow managed to only break one minor one in the course of your life, it still would be enough to keep you out of Heaven.

The Bible never teaches that good people go to Heaven; it teaches that *forgiven* people go to Heaven.

Sins of Omission

Did you know there are sins of both *commission* and *omission*?

I heard about a Sunday school teacher who was trying to explain that concept to her class. She said, "Kids, today we want to talk about the sins of commission and omission. Who can tell me what the sin of commission is?"

A little girl sitting near the front of the class said, "I know the answer. That's when you do something you shouldn't do."

"Very good," said the teacher. "Now, who can tell me what the sin of omission is?"

A boy in the back of the room waved his hand back and forth, and the teacher called on him. "Okay," she said, "what is the sin of omission?"

"Those are sins you want to do," he said, "but you haven't gotten around to them yet."

Well, not quite.

The sin of commission is doing what you should not do; the sin of omission is *not* doing what you *should* do. The point is that we have all sinned in one way or another.

Jesus was seeking to point out this fact to this rich ruler, but the young man seemed full of himself, and the truth wasn't sinking in.

After he essentially told the Lord, "Yes, yes, I've done all that," Jesus issued a challenge to him:

> "If you want to give it all you've got," Jesus replied, "go sell your possessions; give everything to the poor. All your wealth will then be in heaven. Then come follow me."
> (Matthew 19:21, MSG)

By the way, Jesus never said that to *anyone else*. Why did He say it to this particular young man? Because this guy was possessed by his possessions. Money and possessions were his god, and as Jesus told His disciples before,

Chapter 8: **The Pursuit of Happiness**

"You cannot serve both God and money" (Luke 16:13, NIV).

Everyone has a god—including atheists and agnostics. Everyone has some altar they bow before. Your god might be your stuff. Your god might be a relationship. Your god might be success. But here is the all-important question: Can your god save you in the last day of your life?

Your possessions won't save you. Your relationships won't save you. Your credit cards won't save you. Your investments won't save you. Even the gold you have tucked away in that safe won't save you. Only God can save you.

The problem with the young man in Matthew 19 was that he was possessed by all his stuff. Jesus knew that he could never enter into a relationship with the living God until he let go of those possessions. Jesus was saying, "I can see in your heart that you really want to know Me. So take the plunge! Cut that stuff loose and come along with Me. Do it now!"

This young man was tragically held back from a relationship with God by the things he possessed.

What's holding you back from Jesus Christ? Maybe you've put off giving your life to Christ because you're afraid of what others might think about you. You'll have to forget about that, because the more important question is, what does God think? One day you will stand all alone before God, and you won't have your friends there for moral support. God will ask you one question: "What did you do with My Son, Jesus Christ?"

When I became a Christian in high school, it was a huge surprise to everyone. It wasn't long before my friends didn't want to be part of my life anymore. And the truth was, I really didn't want to be part of their lives, because I knew the direction they were headed, and I knew that led to nowhere. In fact, it was leading to misery and ultimately to Hell.

There comes a point when you have to declare yourself and take a stand. Don't let anything or anyone hold you back from God.

Someone might ask, "Greg, do I have to give up anything to follow Jesus Christ?"

Yes. You have to give up emptiness. You have to give up misery. You have to give up guilt. You have to give up the fear of death.

And in the place of those, God will give you fulfillment, happiness, inner peace, and the guaranteed hope of Heaven. It is God's trade-in deal, and you'll never find another one like it.

A Contrast of Two Lives

We've been looking at the story of a wealthy young man who ended up making a tragic decision, affecting not only the rest of his life but perhaps his eternity as well. (If he ever changed his mind about Jesus, the Bible doesn't tell us.)

But the Scriptures talk about another wealthy man who heard the same message and made a very different decision. This was a man who had come all the way from Ethiopia. In fact, he was a high government official of that nation and worked directly with the Queen of Ethiopia.

Like the rich young ruler, he also felt an emptiness in his heart. He had traveled all the way to Jerusalem searching for God, but he hadn't found Him. So he was riding home in his chariot with his entourage, wondering where the answer to life might be.

At least he continued looking in the right place! The book of Acts tells us that as he rode along on his way back to Ethiopia, he was searching the Scriptures for answers. God had directed a man named Philip to meet him on the desert highway and share Christ with him.

The Ethiopian man was delighted, and he believed in Jesus right on the spot. After he and Phillip parted company, the Bible tells us that the Ethiopian "went on his way rejoicing" (Acts 8:39).

So let's look at these men in contrast. Two successful, wealthy men come to Jesus. One goes away sad, and the other goes away glad. We all face the same choice in life: What will we do with Jesus Christ?

A Final Story

I read the story of a very wealthy man who, along with his son, had a passion for collecting fine art. They had priceless paintings and other works of art adorning the walls and shelves of their massive family estate. The nation was at war at that time, and along with so many thousands of others, the young man went to serve his country.

After a number of weeks, the father received a message that his son had been killed in the line of duty.

The Christmas holidays came, and the wealthy father was heartbroken. The joy of the season had vanished with the death of his son. On Christmas morning, there was a knock at his door that woke him up. He opened the door, and there stood a soldier with a large package in his hands.

"Sir," the soldier said, "I was a friend of your son's. In fact, I was the one he was saving when he was killed in the line of duty. Sir, I'd like to come in for a moment if I could."

The father invited this young soldier in, and they sat together by the fireplace. Immediately, the soldier began unwrapping the package. It was a painting of the wealthy man's son. It wasn't what you'd call a great work of art, but the young soldier had somehow managed to capture the slain soldier's face.

Deeply moved, the father stood up and took down the priceless painting that had been hanging over the fireplace, replacing it with the portrait of his son. As the days went by, he would just sit there in his chair and stare at that painting of the boy he loved so much.

A year later the man died, and the art world was abuzz because everyone was anticipating the upcoming auction. According to the man's will, all of his artwork would be auctioned off on Christmas day—the very day he had received the best Christmas present ever.

Soon the room was filled with art collectors and speculators from all over the world. This would be a day when dreams would be fulfilled. The auction began, however, with a painting that wasn't on anyone's museum list. It was a painting of the man's son. The auctioneer asked for an opening bid, but the room was silent.

"Who will open the bidding with $100?"

No one spoke.

Finally someone yelled out, "Who cares about that stupid painting? It's just a picture of his son. Let's get to the real art."

"No," the auctioneer responded, "we have to sell this one first. Who will take the son?"

There was a neighbor who knew the boy. He said, "I'll give you fifty dollars for it. I knew the boy, and I'd like to have it."

The auctioneer said, "Going once. Going twice. Gone." The gavel fell, and cheers filled the room.

Someone shouted, "Let's get on to the *real* auction now."

But then the auctioneer surprised everyone. Looking out over the crowd, he calmly stated, "The auction is officially over."

Everyone was stunned. Someone said, "What do you mean it's over? We didn't come here for the stupid painting of this man's son. There is art available here worth millions of dollars. What's going on?"

"It's very simple," the auctioneer replied. "According to the will of the father, whoever takes the son gets it all."

The fact is that you can spend your life chasing after all the glittering things this world has to offer that promise happiness.

Or, you can take the Son.

If you believe in Jesus, you get it all: purpose, meaning, inner peace, joy that bubbles up from the inside, and—best of all—the hope of Heaven when you leave this life.

WHAT DO
YOU LIVE FOR?

What do you get up and out of bed for each and every day? As someone has put it, is it an alarm clock or a calling that gets you out of bed? What gets your blood pumping? What do you think about the most?

The truth is that most people have no idea.

A poll was done on the Oprah Winfrey show. The famous television hostess had asked the question "What is your life passion?"

Of those polled, a full 70 percent had no idea. Most were simply enduring—instead of enjoying—their lives.

The favorite word for a great many people is *someday*. Someday they will build that dream house. Someday they will find that perfect relationship. Someday their prince (or princess) will come.

But here's the thing most people don't plan on. They don't plan on death. Why in the world not? I don't know why it comes as a shock to us.

A salesperson trying to sell you a life insurance policy will talk about the benefits that your family will receive "if something should happen" to you.

If? If something should happen?

It's not a matter of if but when.

The statistics on death, after all, are pretty impressive: one out of every one person will die.

But we don't like to think about that, do we? We don't even like to use that word *death*. Even so, we have to face our own mortality.

Actor Michael Douglas survived stage four throat cancer. He did an interview with *USA Today* after discovering that he had cancer. The article pointed out that the actor had not pondered the meaning of life yet or undertaken any "soul-searching journeys to faraway lands." Douglas told the interviewer, "I like my odds. I'm not dealing with any mortality issues until they tell me, 'Oops, we have to go back and do surgery,' or something like that." He went on to say, "I haven't found God yet."[1]

I hope that he does find God. I hope that this actor will finally come to grips with his mortality. Douglas is like so many today who don't want to deal with the issue of death until they absolutely have to. We try to shut the whole reality of death out of our minds because it terrifies us.

In a recent interview Woody Allen spoke about his own mortality and was asked how he felt about the aging process.

"I am against it," he replied. Then he went on to say, "You don't gain any wisdom as the years go by. You fall apart, is what happens. . . . I've experienced that thing where you wake up in the middle of the night and you start to think about your own mortality and envision it, and it gives you a little shiver."[2]

Has that happened to you? Eventually it is something that each one of us will have to face because death comes to every person and knocks on every door. The Bible says there is a time to be born and a time to die (see Ecclesiastes 3:2). On a worldwide scale, says author Randy Alcorn, "3 people die every second, 180 every minute, and nearly 11,000 every hour."[3]

Memento Mori

In days gone by people spoke more about death than they do today. You can easily see that in songs, hymns, and poems from centuries past. Ancient merchants would write the words *Memento mori*—"remember that you must die"—in large letters on the first page of their accounting books. Philip of Macedon, father of Alexander the Great, commissioned his servants to stand in his presence every day and say, "Philip, you will die."

And then that day came—unexpectedly—at the hands of an assassin.

In contrast, France's Louis the IX decreed that the word *death* could not even be used in his presence. Frankly, a lot of us are more like Louis than we are like Philip.

And then it hits.

It hit me hard when my son Christopher died in an automobile accident. This is something that you never expect, never plan for, and never dream in your worst nightmare. We know that our grandparents will die, we know that our parents will die, and we may even be conscious of the fact that our older siblings will die. But you never plan on your children dying.

When I heard the news that my firstborn son was no longer on this earth, it was like the world stopped and every bit of air was sucked out of the room. I felt such pain and anguish that I thought I would die right there on the spot.

But I also have to add something else to that account. There, in that worst moment of my life, God was with me. And He took me through that deep darkness. I would never paint a rosy picture of those days and say that it was easy.

It wasn't easy. It isn't easy now. Christians mourn as much as anyone else. We miss our loved ones. The Bible speaks of "a time to weep, and a time to laugh; a time to mourn, and a time to dance" (Ecclesiastes 3:4).

Even so, I have never doubted for even one moment that my son is in the presence of God in Heaven because he had placed his faith in Jesus Christ. That is the hope of every believer. Christopher Laurie isn't in Heaven because he was Greg and Cathe Laurie's child; he is in Heaven because he was God's child and had said yes to Jesus.

So What Do You Live For?

Not everyone would know how to answer the question "What do you live for?" in a succinct way. But the apostle Paul had no problem at all. And he summed it up like this: "For to me, to live is Christ, and to die is gain" (Philippians 1:21).

Paul, in a Roman prison as he penned these words, went on to say, "But if I live, I can do more fruitful work for Christ. So I really don't know which is better. I'm torn between two desires: I long to go and be with Christ, which would be far better for me. But for your sakes, it is better that I continue to live" (verses 22–24, NLT).

It's obvious what drove Paul's life.

What is it that drives your life?

PEOPLE WHO LIVE "JUST TO LIVE"

Everyone lives for someone or something. Some people live just to live. Their philosophy would be, "Hey, man, take it easy. Chill. Take it a day at a time." These people feel they are nothing more than a highly evolved animal. In their blinded minds, there is no afterlife, no Heaven, no Hell, no final judgment. There is just the here and now. As Henry David Thoreau wrote, "You must live in the present . . . find your eternity in each moment. Fools stand on their island opportunities and look toward another land. There is no other land; there is no other life but this, or the like of this."[4]

These are people who live for the moment and are determined to satisfy their desires, no matter how bizarre or deviant they might be. The apostle Paul spoke in Philippians 3:19 about those who live for their appetites alone, "whose god is their belly." (And for some people, their "god" is a little bigger than others!)

If you try to bring up spiritual issues with these people, they don't want to think about it. "I don't want to get into that," they will say. Or, "I'm not interested." For them, to live is just to live.

PEOPLE WHO LIVE FOR PLEASURE

Others, however, believe that life is all about pleasure. It's to have fun. Get the buzz. Feel the rush. Have the experience. The problem with this, however, is that these experiences are so short-lived.

Let me say something here that you will rarely hear a preacher say. Sin really can be fun.

I didn't say that sin was good; I'm just admitting the simple fact that it can be fun—for a very brief time. And then payday comes.

If you jumped off the top of the Willis Tower in Chicago, there certainly would be a rush—until you hit the ground. If you live for pleasure, it's a lot like going to an amusement park such as Disneyland or Walt Disney World. You stand in line and wait and wait and wait for your turn. Then the attendant buckles you in, the ride lasts for about forty seconds, and you're through.

That's what living for pleasure is like. You wait for your chance, you have the pleasure and feel the buzz, and then it's over. And the repercussions start rolling in. What a waste. The Bible says that "she who lives in pleasure is dead while she lives" (1 Timothy 5:6).

Have you ever felt that? Have you ever felt the deadness, even in the midst of supposedly having a good time?

Before I was a Christian, I used to drink, party, and do drugs. But there were times when I would be sitting at some party, surrounded by laughing people, and say to myself, "I hate this. I'm not having fun. This is empty."

PEOPLE WHO LIVE FOR FIGHTS AND ARGUMENTS

Then there would be some who would say, "To live is to get even!" Their motto in life is "Don't get mad, get even!" They live for the fight. They live for the argument. They spin elaborate daydreams about what they will say or what they will do or how they will feel when they get revenge on someone who has hurt or offended them.

PEOPLE WHO LIVE FOR POSSESSIONS

The philosophy here is a familiar one: he who dies with the most toys wins. These are the people who have to get the latest, biggest, fastest, newest, and shiniest, whatever it is.

This is nothing new, of course. Millennia ago, King Solomon, the wealthiest man of his time, had everything a man could ever desire. He recorded some of his observations on that lifestyle in Ecclesiastes, an autobiographical book he wrote as he was running from God:

> I also tried to find meaning by building huge homes for myself and by planting beautiful vineyards. I made gardens and parks, filling them with all kinds of fruit trees. I built reservoirs to collect the water to irrigate my many flourishing groves. . . . I also owned large herds and flocks. . . . I collected great sums of silver and gold, the treasure of many kings and provinces . . . and had many beautiful concubines. I had everything a man could desire . . .
>
> But as I looked at everything I had worked so hard to accomplish, it was all so meaningless—like chasing the wind. There was nothing really worthwhile anywhere.
>
> (2:4–8,11, NLT)

You might say, "Oh Greg, that was ancient history. If Solomon lived today and had all that stuff, he would never say that."

On the contrary, I think he would.

Multimillionaire Simon Cowell, one of the most successful men in show business today, was interviewed in his 14,000-square-foot home, complete with staff, guest house, movie theater, and a garage that houses a Rolls Royce, a Bentley, a Ferrari, and other cars like that. Surely a man in a situation like that would have a lot to be happy about. But here is what he said in the interview: "I get in very dark moods for no reason. Nothing in particular brings it on. You can be having the best time of your life and yet you're utterly and totally miserable."

He went on to say, "I am just a wandering asteroid without a home. I get to points in my life where I sometimes think I'm never going to be happy. Someone said to me recently, 'You're like a human buffet table. Everyone comes and takes something from you and, at the end, there's nothing left.' "[5]

Wow. He sounds just like Solomon, doesn't he?

Have you come to a conclusion like that?

PEOPLE WHO LIVE FOR KNOWLEDGE

Maybe you would say, "No, I don't really live for pleasure or possessions. I live to acquire knowledge. I'm an academic, and I love to study."

That's certainly commendable. But if in your pursuit of great knowledge you forget about God, even that will be an empty search. Again, here is what Solomon wrote—a man regarded as the wisest man who ever lived:

> I, the Teacher, was king of Israel, and I lived in Jerusalem. I devoted myself to search for understanding and to explore by wisdom everything being done under heaven. . . . I said to myself, "Look, I am wiser than any of the kings who ruled in Jerusalem before me. I have greater wisdom and knowledge than any of them." So I set out

to learn everything from wisdom to madness and folly. But I learned firsthand that pursuing all this is like chasing the wind.

> The greater my wisdom, the greater my grief.
> To increase knowledge only increases sorrow.

(Ecclesiastes 1:12–13,16–18, NLT)

That might be a good verse for kids to quote to their parents the next time Mom or Dad sends them to their room to do their homework. "*Mom, the Bible says that 'to increase knowledge only increases sorrow.' I'm going to go play video games now.*"

Not long before he died, the brilliant physicist Robert Oppenheimer thought he was a complete failure. Oppenheimer had held a leadership role in the Manhattan Project, the research team that produced the atomic bomb, and also served as the head of the Institute for Advanced Study at Princeton. In retrospect he said of all his accomplishments, "They leave on the tongue only the taste of ashes."[6]

To live for possessions or pleasure or even the pursuit of knowledge will leave you empty, empty, empty.

IN CONTRAST . . .

The apostle Paul knew exactly what he was living for. In one of his letters from a Roman prison he wrote, "For to me, to live is Christ, and to die is gain" (Philippians 1:21).

Why was Paul so sure that dying and going to Heaven was gain? Because he had already been there! Earlier in his life, Paul had the unique experience of dying, departing for Heaven, and coming back to Earth. He didn't write a lot about the experience. What little he said about it came out in his letter to the Corinthians:

> Fourteen years ago I was taken up to heaven for a visit. Don't ask me whether my body was there or just my spirit, for I don't know; only God can answer that. But anyway, there I was in paradise, and heard things so astounding that they are beyond a man's power to describe or put in words (and anyway I am not allowed to tell them to others). That experience is something worth bragging about, but I am not going to do it.
> (2 Corinthians 12:2–5, TLB)

Can you imagine what that would have been like?

It was as though the Lord had said to him, "Welcome, Paul. I have some good news and some bad news."

"What's the good news, Lord?"

"You will *come back again.*"

"And the bad news?"

"Some people are praying for you to be raised from the dead back on Earth."

"Oh no! Don't listen to them, Lord!"

Who could blame him for being a little upset about that? Listen, if I die and enter Heaven, I don't want anyone praying that I'll be raised from the dead. Once I'm on the other side with Jesus, there is no way I'd want to return to the trials and tribulations of life on Earth.

Paul went on to tell the Philippians, in effect, "I'm torn. I really want to be back in Heaven again, but I know I still have work to do here on earth. So I'm okay with that, but being with Christ would be better by far!" (see Philippians 1:22–25). Death didn't frighten Paul because he knew where he was going.

You and I don't have to be afraid of death, either. It doesn't mean that you look forward to it, and it doesn't mean that you have a death wish. It simply means that you don't have to dread or fear it if you have put your faith in Jesus Christ. If you haven't put your faith in Jesus Christ, then you certainly *should* be scared to death of death because there is a judgment waiting for the person who does not believe.

Back in Philippians 1:23, Paul wrote about "having a desire to depart and be with Christ." The term translated *depart* is an interesting word in the original language. It could be translated "to strike the tent."

Speaking for myself, I've never been a big fan of camping. My favorite part of the whole experience is breaking camp and heading home.

The Bible, then, compares the human body to a tent. What an appropriate metaphor! Sometimes we might fool ourselves into believing that the body is a permanent residence, but it's not. It's a tent. It's temporary.

Now, you can take your temporary tent body and do all manner of cosmetic things to it. You can color it, stretch it, tattoo it, and inject things into it in an effort to make yourself look younger or more stylish. Just remember that all of those so-called improvements are temporary cosmetic changes to a temporary, fading structure.

In the book of 2 Corinthians, Paul put it like this:

> For we know that if the earthly tent we live in is destroyed, we have a building from God, an eternal house in heaven, not built by human hands. Meanwhile we groan, longing to be clothed instead with our heavenly dwelling, because when we are clothed, we will not be found naked. For while we are in this tent, we groan and are burdened, because we do not wish to be unclothed but to be clothed instead with our heavenly dwelling, so that what is mortal may be swallowed up by life. (5:1–4, NIV)

I mentioned that the word Paul used for *depart* could be translated as "strike the tent." But it could also be translated "released from shackles." It could be that you are bound right now as you read these words. You might be incarcerated. Maybe you are in the prison of a body with a severe disability or suffer with chronic pain.

If you know Jesus Christ as Savior, one day you will be free from all such shackles. One day you will fly away into the presence of God. As that classic hymn says,

> Some glad morning when this life is o'er,
> I'll fly away;
> To a home on God's celestial shore,
> I'll fly away.

Another possible translation of that same term used for *depart* describes untying a boat from its moorings. Paul is saying, "The time is coming for me to set sail."

Sometimes when a loved one leaves on a long trip, we might feel sadness. But it really all depends on where they're going, doesn't it? If they are boarding a rusty old freighter to sail to Outer Siberia, I might feel bad for them. But if they are on a beautiful new cruise ship destined for Tahiti, I can't feel bad for them at all (except for myself because I'm still here).

Don't feel sorrow for anyone who has died as a believer in Jesus, because that friend or loved one or coworker of yours is in eternal bliss. But yes, we might very well feel sorrow for ourselves because we miss that person.

Paul says that to be with Christ "is far better."

The Greek word he used for *far better* could be translated "far, far, far better." Why is Heaven better than Earth? It's better because I am moving from a tent to a mansion!

If you happen to be as old as I am, you may remember *The Beverly Hillbillies* television show. In that program, Jed Clampett, Granny, Elly May, and Jethro became millionaires and moved out of their rundown shack in the South to a huge mansion in Beverly Hills, California. No one felt sorry for the Clampetts.

The truth is that one day we will be leaving behind our temporary tent and moving into a mansion. Jesus said, "In My Father's house are many mansions; if it were not so, I would have told you. I go to prepare a place for you" (John 14:2).

Was He speaking of a literal mansion, or was He speaking of the new, made-to-live-forever body that we will receive in Heaven? I don't know. But I do know that it will be better—better by far.

The older you become, the more you realize these things. My generation, the baby boomers, are having trouble with aging. One of our favorite theme songs was "Forever Young," and we really don't want to admit that we're getting old.

One article I read said, "Baby boomers, the original architects of the youth culture, . . . launched sit-ins and love-ins, as well as the careers of Elvis, The Rolling Stones and other symbols of rebellion. Now instead of sex, drugs and rock 'n' roll, it's nip, tuck and Botox."[7]

We have gone from acid rock to acid reflux.

Heaven is better than Earth because all of our questions will be answered—and I do have questions. One of the things you inevitably ask when a tragedy hits is why. Why someone so young? Why so much suffering? Frankly it doesn't make sense to me. I don't agree with it. I don't like it. But I do trust God and know deep down in my heart that He is in control. And I know that one day, all of these issues will be resolved.

By the way, there's nothing wrong with asking God why. But don't necessarily expect an answer—at least not in this life. But one day we will have the answer.

I heard about a woman who was throwing a dinner party. Turning to her little six-year-old daughter, she asked her if she would say the blessing.

"But Mommy," the little girl said, "I don't know what to say."

Her mom told her, "Well, just pray what you always hear mommy say."

So the little girl prayed, "Lord, why on earth did I invite all of these people to dinner?"

One day all our questions—even ones like that—will be answered. In 1 Corinthians 13:12 Paul wrote, "Now I know in part; then I shall know fully, even as I am fully known" (NIV). In other words, we will know with perfect clarity.

The best thing of all about going to Heaven is that I will be with Christ—forever. D. L. Moody once said that it is not the jeweled walls and pearly gates that will make Heaven attractive. It is being with God.

You don't go to Heaven to find Christ; you go to Christ to find Heaven. Again, Paul wrote, "For to me, to live is Christ, and to die is gain" (Philippians 1:21).

But what if you live for money? Then to die is to leave it all behind.

What if you live for fame? Then to die is to be forgotten.

What if you live for power? Then to die is to lose it all.

But if you say "to live is Christ," then you have Him both right now and for all eternity.

Do you know Him?

He is alive, and He is ready to come into your life.

Chapter

YOU MUST
BE BORN AGAIN

There are certain things in life that most of us "just know."

In my early years there was a popular song by Jim Croce that spoke to the things he thought people ought to know. He sang, "You don't tug on Superman's cape, you don't spit into the wind, you don't pull the mask off the old Lone Ranger, and you don't mess around with Jim."

We all know some basic stuff about life. But sometimes I wonder if we really know as much as we *think* we know.

Those of us who claim to know the Bible, and particularly the New Testament, would all say that we're very familiar with the contents of the third chapter of the gospel of John: Nicodemus, the teacher who came to Jesus by night, and the Lord's strong declaration, "You must be born again."

Maybe we've become so familiar with the story that we skim right over it when we're reading the Bible. But by not looking carefully at this important account and conversation in the Scriptures, we might miss an essential truth of life—both this life and the next.

A Late-Night Conversation

In this message we will consider a nighttime conversation between Jesus and a man named Nicodemus. (I almost called this chapter "Nick at Night" but decided against it.)

In the Israel of that day, Nicodemus was about as respected and respectable as a man could be. He was deeply religious, devout, pious, moral, educated, wealthy, and famous. But even with all of that going for him, there was something missing in his life, and he knew it. Risking his own reputation and standing in the religious community, he sought out the young rabbi from Galilee. He *had* to talk to Jesus, period.

You might wonder what possible relevance a two-thousand-year-old talk between a religious leader in Israel and the son of a carpenter might have for you today, with all the complexities and stresses of our contemporary world and the cares and concerns of your own life.

Well, actually it has a lot to do with you.

This wasn't just a conversation between two men; for all practical purposes, this was a conversation between a man and God.

We know that Jesus Himself is God, but what about the other side of that dialogue? How did Nicodemus stack up as a representative of humanity in an encounter with God Almighty?

Answer: Surprisingly well.

Nicodemus was a good man, relatively speaking, and Jesus even acknowledged him as the teacher of Israel. But

Chapter 10: **You Must Be Born Again**

his life was incomplete. And apart from what Jesus had to offer that night, so is ours.

Setting the Table

As you might anticipate, the final verses of John 2 really set the table for John 3. Let's take a quick step back in order to gain more of the context. In John 2:23 we read,

> Now when He was in Jerusalem at the Passover, during the feast, many believed in His name when they saw the signs which He did.

That sounds good. People are witnessing Jesus' power and miracles and are believing in His name. But then note what John wrote in the very next verses:

> But Jesus did not commit Himself to them, because He knew all men, and had no need that anyone should testify of man, for He knew what was in man. (verses 24-25)

Here's how these last verses read in *The Message* paraphrase: "But Jesus didn't entrust his life to them. He knew them inside and out, knew how untrustworthy they were. He didn't need any help in seeing right through them."

In other words, they believed in Him, but He didn't believe in them.

Why?

Because Jesus, being omniscient (all-knowing), saw that their faith was not genuine but shallow and superficial. In fact, there are many people like that today. They say they believe in Jesus, they say they trust in Him, but they may be fooling others—or even fooling themselves.

But you can't fool God. You can fool all of the people some of the time, you can fool some of the people all of the time, but you can't fool God any of the time.

If you are a true seeker, if you really want to know God, He will show you the answers. Jeremiah 29:13 says, "And you will seek Me and find Me, when you search for Me with all your heart." James 4:8 assures us, "Come near to God and he will come near to you" (NIV).

Nicodemus was a true seeker. He really wanted to know. He really wanted to understand. And he came to exactly the right Person: the living, breathing, very Son of God.

As Bible teacher G. Campbell Morgan has pointed out, this conversation has three essential movements: face to face in verses 2–3, mind to mind in verses 4–8, and finally, heart to heart in verses 9–21:[1]

> There was a man of the Pharisees named Nicodemus, a ruler of the Jews. This man came to Jesus by night and said to Him, "Rabbi, we know that You are a teacher come from God; for no one can do these signs that You do unless God is with him."
>
> Jesus answered and said to him, "Most assuredly, I say to you, unless one is born again, he cannot see the kingdom of God."

Nicodemus said to Him, "How can a man be born when he is old? Can he enter a second time into his mother's womb and be born?"

Jesus answered, "Most assuredly, I say to you, unless one is born of water and the Spirit, he cannot enter the kingdom of God. That which is born of the flesh is flesh, and that which is born of the Spirit is spirit. Do not marvel that I said to you, 'You must be born again.' The wind blows where it wishes, and you hear the sound of it, but cannot tell where it comes from and where it goes. So is everyone who is born of the Spirit."

Nicodemus answered and said to Him, "How can these things be?"

Jesus answered and said to him, "Are you the teacher of Israel, and do not know these things? Most assuredly, I say to you, We speak what We know and testify what We have seen, and you do not receive Our witness. If I have told you earthly things and you do not believe, how will you believe if I tell you heavenly things? No one has ascended to heaven but He who came down from heaven, that is, the Son of Man who is in heaven. And as Moses lifted up the serpent in the wilderness, even so must the Son of Man be lifted up, that whoever believes in Him should not perish but have eternal life. For God so loved the world that He gave His only begotten Son, that whoever

believes in Him should not perish but have ever-lasting life."
(John 3:1–16)

"You Must Be Born Again"

Jesus said to Nicodemus, "*You must be born again.*" What a powerful statement that is. What did Jesus actually mean by that strong declaration?

Being born again certainly gives us the idea of a major change in life. It speaks of a fresh start, a new beginning, and even starting over again.

Obviously we are a culture that is obsessed with change. Fashions change. Musical styles change. Programming changes. We are constantly looking for the next new thing. What's cool? What's hip? What's the latest trend?

Change appeals to people. They find themselves thinking, *If I just had a new house . . . a new face . . . a new job . . . a new spouse, I would finally be happy.* We love the idea of starting over again in life.

I wonder, however, if we even understand what this phrase "born again" really means. According to research conducted by the Barna Group, almost one-third of America's teenagers claim to be "born again."

Are they?

Of those who say they are born again, 60 percent believe that "the Bible is totally accurate in all of its teachings." This means that 40 percent of those who claim born again status don't necessarily believe the Bible is totally accurate.

It gets even worse. Within this same group of supposedly born again American teens, "slightly more than half . . . believe that Jesus committed sins while he was on the earth," 60 percent think that "enough good works" will get them into Heaven, and almost two-thirds "say that Satan is just a symbol of evil and not a living being." Only 6 percent believe there are moral absolutes.[2]

And according to Josh McDowell, nearly 60 percent of evangelical Christian teens "now say that 'all religious faiths teach equally valid truths.'"[3]

So what's going on here? All these people claim to be born again, yet their belief system seems to contradict what that would imply.

Here is what it comes down to. The very phrase "born again" has been pirated and emptied of its meaning. It has been dragged through the gutter and given back to us minus its power. Today when people say they are born again, many—and perhaps most—really have no idea what they are talking about.

Jesus, however, will settle the issue for us right here in John 3. He will tell us that we must be born again, and He will tell us what it means to be born again.

A Portrait of Nicodemus

Who was this heart-hungry Jewish leader who came to Jesus by night?

First of all, we are told in verse 1 that he was a Pharisee. Generally when we think of Pharisees, we see them in a negative light. We remember that our Lord saved His most scathing words for the scribes, Pharisees, and religious leaders. We tend to think that all of these men were hypocrites, but that isn't necessarily the case.

Actually, to be a Pharisee was somewhat commendable. A Pharisee was a member of a select group that never numbered more than six thousand. Each person who became a Pharisee had to take a solemn vow before three witnesses that he would devote every moment of his life to obeying the Ten Commandments. Pharisees took the Law of God very seriously and sought to apply the Ten Commandments in every area of their lives.

The problem, however, was that they weren't satisfied with the Scriptures alone and wanted rules of life and conduct to be spelled out much more specifically. In response to this, a group of people arose from within the ranks of the Pharisees, calling themselves "scribes." Their job was to spell out how the Ten Commandments applied to every area of life—and they took their job *very* seriously. As a result of their work, they compiled a thick book of additional laws, rules, and regulations that the Jews have to this day. It's called the Mishnah.

How thorough is this book of rules? It devotes twenty-four chapters alone to not working on the Sabbath! In addition to this volume, the scribes wrote a commentary on the Mishnah called the Talmud. These super-religious Jews, then, would spend their lives poring over these volumes and studying them in great detail. That is what Nicodemus essentially did with his life.

But Nicodemus wasn't just a Pharisee; John tells us that he was a *leader* of the Pharisees, which means that he would have been a member of the elite seventy-member Sanhedrin, the ruling body or "supreme court" for the Jewish nation. Unlike our Supreme Court in the United States today, however, the Sanhedrin intertwined politics and religion, making religious as well as judicial rulings over the lives of the people.

So picture Nicodemus as he perhaps climbed the steps of the house where Jesus was staying and met Him on the flat rooftop veranda. He was knowledgeable, respectable, and probably something of a celebrity in his city and country. When Jesus said to him, "Are you the teacher of Israel, and do not know these things?" it implies that Nicodemus was known by everyone, and his name probably was a household word. He was a man whom others looked to, respected, and sought out for his opinions and thoughts on various matters.

But as I have said, something was missing in this man's life.

He was searching, and something in him told Nicodemus that this young rabbi Jesus might have the answers he was seeking in life.

We are told in John 3:2 that he came to Jesus by night. Why does the Bible mention the time of day when he made his call? We can only speculate. Perhaps he was afraid to be seen by others seeking out Jesus. After all, he was very well known and might have feared the criticism or scorn of others.

It's not by accident that the Bible compares people with sheep. Sheep tend to simply follow one another—even if it is in the wrong direction. I read an article in the paper about 1,500 sheep that literally walked off a cliff in Turkey. Of that number, 450 of them died, and the rest survived because their fall was cushioned by the animals that had already strolled off the cliff's edge.[4]

Why did they all walk off a cliff? It's not complicated. One sheep walked in that direction, and the others (not having anything better to do) just followed along. It's as though the sheep were saying to each other, "Okay, guys. Get in a single line. We're all going to die today. Everybody line up and keep moving. Let's go! Let's go! It's not that *baaaad!*"

The Bible says, "All we like sheep have gone astray; we have turned, every one, to his own way" (Isaiah 53:6). That's a portrait of every one of us in our humanity.

Nicodemus might have been somewhat sheeplike in the beginning, but in the end he turned out to be one of the bravest followers of Jesus. You have to start somewhere! Some have an outwardly impressive beginning in the faith, only to deny Him or wander away from Him later in life. Nicodemus was just making his way into the kingdom while Judas Iscariot was seemingly a full-fledged apostle in good standing. In the end Judas betrayed our Lord for thirty pieces of silver and then went out and hung himself. Nicodemus, however, publicly stood for Christ.

In John 19 we read these words:

After all this, Joseph of Arimathea (he was a disciple of Jesus, but secretly, because he was intimidated by the Jews) petitioned Pilate to take the body of Jesus. Pilate gave permission. So Joseph came and took the body.

Nicodemus, who had first come to Jesus at night, came now in broad daylight carrying a mixture of myrrh and aloes, about seventy-five pounds. They took Jesus' body and, following the Jewish burial custom, wrapped it in linen with the spices. There was a garden near the place he was crucified, and in the garden a new tomb in which no one had yet been placed. So, because it was Sabbath preparation for the Jews and the tomb was convenient, they placed Jesus in it.

(verses 38–42, MSG)

I love that it points out that Nicodemus came out publicly for Christ in the end. He may have first come to Jesus at night, but in the end he identified with Jesus in broad daylight. It's so much better to have a feeble beginning and a strong finish than a strong beginning and no finish.

If you have fallen in your walk with God, it is time to get back in the race. It's all about finishing.

Face to Face

Finally the moment came for their conversation. Nicodemus sat down with God in human form and began to open up his heart.

He said, "Rabbi, we know that You are a teacher come from God; for no one can do these signs that You do unless God is with him" (John 3:2).

That alone was quite an admission. For a man like Nicodemus to call Jesus "rabbi" meant that he was humbling himself before Him.

Can you imagine how nervous Nicodemus must have been? He had an appointment with Jesus. He may have recited his lines over and over before he stepped into the Lord's presence. Calling Jesus "rabbi" was an important admission and acknowledgement for him.

Perhaps it's the same for you as you encounter this message. You have some good impressions of the believers in your life. They might seem a little weird to you, but on the whole they are honest, considerate, and friendly. You have always respected Jesus Christ as a great moral teacher. That's how Nicodemus felt as he began feeling his way into this conversation.

But Jesus cut right to the chase.

"*You must be born again.*"

With a single sharp and penetrating phrase, Jesus sliced through all the layers of rules and legalistic attitudes that had accumulated around the mind of Nicodemus. Like a sword, these simple words pierced this Pharisee's heart.

"*You must be born again.*"

In the New King James Version, Jesus prefaced His statement by saying, "Most assuredly, I say to you." In the King James Version, it says, "Verily, verily, I say unto thee."

In *The Living Bible* it says, "With all the earnestness I possess I tell you this."

The idea is that Jesus was saying to Nicodemus, "I'm going to reveal to you a fundamental reality of life, so listen carefully. This is not an option. This is absolute. This is required. You must be born again. Why? Because if you aren't born again, you will not enter the kingdom of God."

C. S. Lewis, the author of *The Chronicles of Narnia* series and a great Christian thinker, said,

> A man who was merely a man and said the sort of things Jesus said would not be a great moral teacher. He would either be a lunatic—on a level with a man who says he is a poached egg—or else he would be the Devil of Hell. . . . You can shut Him up for a fool, you can spit at Him and kill Him as a demon, or you can fall at His feet and call Him Lord and God. But let us not come with any patronizing nonsense about His being a great human teacher. He has not left that open to us. He did not intend to.[5]

Mind to Mind

Jesus certainly had the Pharisee's attention at this point. Nicodemus was fully engaged:

> "How can a man be born when he is old? Can he enter a second time into his mother's womb and be born?" (John 3:4)

Nicodemus was essentially saying, "Lord, I accept what You say in premise, but . . . how can I start over again? Is it really possible to be born all over again? Obviously you can't enter into your mother's womb after you've grown up. So what are You talking about here?"

Whatever age you may be, the older you become, the more difficult it is to change your ways. This can be shown by the way kids and adults approach Disneyland. When you're young, you want to go on the fastest, most radical ride in the park. When you're older, you say, "When do we eat?" When you're young, you run to the next ride. You see the sign that says IF YOU ARE HERE IN THE LINE, YOU WILL BE ON THE RIDE OF THE MONTH. When you are older, you say, "Where can I take a nap?"

Jesus told Nicodemus what he needed to know. In other words, "Nicodemus, I'm going to give you the most important information you will ever hear: you must be born again."

Again, this term has been diluted and has lost its meaning. People throw it around a lot. We hear people talk about born again this and born again that. Someone can even get involved in New Age mysticism and say they are "born again."

But what does it really mean?

It means that you have had your spiritual eyes opened and have embraced Christ as your Savior and Lord.

This is why you can't explain a nonbeliever into the kingdom. God has to touch him or her.

"Listen to Me, Nicodemus." Jesus was saying. "You need to be born from above. Your religious beliefs aren't going to do it for you. You may be at the top of the heap in the religious world, but it hasn't brought you any closer to Heaven."

Let me make a statement that some might find controversial. I think religion has kept more people out of Heaven than all other sins combined. When I say "religion," I'm talking about man's attempt to reach God.

I don't consider myself to be a religious person.

"What are you talking about?" some might protest. "You're a pastor, a preacher, an evangelist. You're a very religious person!"

I hope not. I certainly try not to be. I don't like religion. In fact, I hate it. Why? Because it blinds people to their need for God. You try to talk to someone about their faith in Christ, and they will say things like this.

"Oh, I was raised a Baptist."

"I grew up as a Presbyterian."

"I'm from a Catholic family."

"I was baptized as a child."

"My grandfather was a preacher."

I feel like saying, "What do you want? A medal?"

Just like the Pharisees, we will go through these little rituals and imagine that we are somehow earning the favor of God. We will hide behind those things in our past—those religious milestones in our lives—and they can actually keep us from a living, dynamic relationship with Jesus Christ. In fact, they can keep us from Heaven.

Besides those things, I think religion makes people weird. I've seen it time and again. Someone "gets religion," and they become unnecessarily critical and judgmental. They can be downright mean. Sometimes they act a little spacey. Whatever they've got, I don't want it. Whatever they claim to have, I'm not interested.

I don't want religion. I have never been enthralled with religious rituals of any kind. When I met God, it was in a personal way. Christ Himself came to live inside of me, and I could never, never deny the reality of that.

I desperately do not want to become a religious person. I want to be a follower of Jesus Christ, and there is a big difference between the two.

When Nicodemus asked, "How can a man be born when he is old?" (John 3:4), I think that was another way of saying, "What's the process here? How does a person start over? Can a man like me really change at this point in life? Really?"

We've all tried to change at one time or another, and we've all experienced frustration over our setbacks and failures. Can a person really change? Can a man or woman become a different person?

We try new clothes. We get a new job. We shed a few pounds. We repaint our car. But what have we really changed, beyond a few externals? I think that was the question that burned in Nicodemus's heart that night as he spoke with the Lord.

I'm imagining that at one point in their dialogue, a cooling breeze swept over the rooftop veranda, perhaps rustling the leaves of a palm tree by the house. Perhaps that prompted the Lord's comment in verse 8: "The wind blows where it wishes, and you hear the sound of it, but cannot tell where it comes from and where it goes. So is everyone who is born of the Spirit."

"Nicodemus," Jesus was saying, "can you see the wind?"

No, you can't. But you do see its effect, don't you? You can feel it on your face and in your hair. You can watch as it rustles the leaves on a tree.

Some people say, "If I can't *see* it, I won't believe it."

But what if you were standing in the middle of a hurricane, watching trees being uprooted and cars flying by? You wouldn't actually see the hurricane, but you could certainly see the effects of the wind.

You may know of someone whose life has been radically changed by a relationship with Christ. Maybe you know a number of such people. That's hard evidence. You might not literally see Jesus Christ operating in their lives, but you have seen the effects of His presence. It's undeniable. You don't *see* the wind, but you see its effect. The same is true when you have been born from above by the Holy Spirit.

Heart to Heart

In verse 9, Nicodemus said to Jesus, "How can these things be?"

In my reading of this passage, I hear some desperation in the Pharisee's voice. It was as though he were saying,

"Yes! I do want this—this born again experience—in my life. I want it badly. But how does it work?"

Jesus shot back with a quick reply: "Are you the teacher of Israel, and do not know these things?" (verse 10). In other words, "Why Nicodemus, you're a famous man. You're respected in this nation. You are well studied. You've spent endless hours in studying the Torah. And you don't understand this?"

Certainly Nicodemus, student of the Scriptures that he was, knew there were passages in the Old Testament that alluded to what our Lord was speaking of when He said, "You must be born again." In Ezekiel 11:19 God says, "I will give them an undivided heart and put a new spirit in them; I will remove from them their heart of stone and give them a heart of flesh" (NIV). That was pointing to a born again experience.

So Jesus was saying, "Nicodemus, this can really happen. You should know this from your study of the Word."

Jesus really laid it out for His nighttime visitor in John 3:14–15: "And as Moses lifted up the serpent in the wilderness, even so must the Son of Man be lifted up, that whoever believes in Him should not perish but have eternal life."

Jesus was sending the famed Pharisee back to the Scriptures, back to the Torah, reminding him of an incident in Numbers 21. The Israelites had been grumbling, complaining, and whining that God had abandoned them. They accused Moses and God of failing them and leaving them to die in the wilderness, and they even began griping about the Lord's provision for them.

As a result of this sin, God sent venomous snakes among them to bite them, and people were dying. Panicked, the people cried out to Moses for help. When Moses went to the Lord about it, God had them set up a tall pole with a brass serpent wrapped around it. Everyone who had been bitten and looked to the serpent, lifted up on high, were saved. Everyone who refused to look died from the venom.

It was a picture of what Christ would one day accomplish for us on the cross. We've all been bitten by the serpent Satan. We have his deadly venom in our system, and it eventually will kill us, separating us from God for eternity. We must quickly find the antidote—which Christ provided for us through His blood, shed on the cross. If we simply will look to Jesus for salvation, we will be forgiven. If we refuse to look to Him in faith, we won't be.

It is as simple as that, and Jesus was pointing Nicodemus to this truth.

And then Jesus brought it all together with what has become the most well-known verse in all the Bible:

> For God so loved the world that He gave His only begotten Son, that whoever believes in Him should not perish but have everlasting life. (John 3:16)

My friend Max Lucado calls John 3:16 "the Hope diamond of the Bible." He writes that this amazing verse is "a twenty-six word parade of hope: beginning with

God, ending with life, and urging us to do the same. Brief enough to write on a napkin or memorize in a moment, yet solid enough to weather two thousand years of storms and questions. If you know nothing of the Bible, start here. If you know everything in the Bible, return here. We all need the reminder."[6] So well said!

This verse has been called the gospel in a nutshell. If you have committed this verse alone to memory, you know enough to do some real damage for the kingdom of God. Why? Because it gives us a remarkable overview of God's plan of salvation.

First of all, it says, "For God so loved . . ."

Some people might say, "For God so hated . . ." They see God as being against humanity, heartlessly choosing some and rejecting others, depending on His whim.

But Jesus said, "For God so loved the world."

He didn't say, "For God so loved the elect" or "For God so loved the chosen few." No, He said *the world*, and that means everyone: every man, every woman, every race and language, and every sinner, no matter what they have done.

Next it says, "That He gave His only begotten Son."

God didn't just talk about His love, He demonstrated it. Romans 5:8 tells us that "God demonstrates his own love for us in this: While we were still sinners, Christ died for us" (NIV). In Romans 6:23 we read, "For the wages of sin is death, but the gift of God is eternal life in Christ Jesus our Lord."

"For God so loved . . . He gave." It is not enough, however, to have someone offer you a gift. You must *accept* it. When someone offers you a gift, you have a choice to either accept it or reject it.

And by the way, when you give a gift with a card to a female, she always will read the card first. Then she will say, "That is so sweet. Thank you." Then she will carefully remove the ribbon from the package, setting it aside and saving it. She somehow opens the package without tearing the paper (which she will also save for later). Then she will open up the box, offering her thanks yet again.

If, however, you give a gift to the average guy, he will open the card to see if there is money in it. Ribbons and wrapping paper are only obstacles to be quickly overcome, and he will rip them off to get at the prize.

Receiving Christ is more than just a matter of believing that He exists. The Bible tells us that even the demons of Hell believe in God and tremble at the thought of Him (see James 2:19).

What does it mean to believe in a biblical sense? It means that not only have you embraced Christ, and Christ alone, for salvation, but you have turned from your sin. Repentance is a part of belief. They're like two sides of a coin.

My fear is there are people who say they have "believed," but they have never repented. Going back to those stats that I mentioned earlier, how can you say you are a Christian and not believe that the Bible is the Word of God? How can you say you are born again and yet believe that Jesus was guilty of sin, which the Bible expressly denies? How can you say that you are a real follower of

Jesus and yet reject what the Bible clearly teaches?

Answer: You can't.

Some will say, "Yes, I'm a Christian. I'm just not one of those 'born agains.' " I hate to break it to these people, but you have to be born again to be a Christian. There is no such thing as a Christian who is not born again.

Jesus said you must be born again. You must believe. And if you believe, He says, you *will* have everlasting life. He doesn't say that you can hope to have eternal life (if God is in a good mood) or that there's an outside chance you will have eternal life. No, Jesus Christ, whose name is Truth, says that you will have it.

This offer is for everyone. The world reaches up to God through ritual and religion. But God reaches down to humanity through Christ. When John 3:16 speaks of "His only begotten Son," this could be better translated as "His one and only Son" or "the only one of its class, unique in kind."

Who can be forgiven? "*Whoever* believes in Him." That means everyone, no matter what they have done and no matter how many sins or how heinous the sins they have committed.

"Whoever believes . . ." What does that mean? It means to put your full trust in Christ. You trust in, cling to, and rely on Christ, and Christ alone, not Christ plus works or Christ plus ritual or Christ plus anything.

"Whoever believes in Him should not perish but have everlasting life." Salvation becomes the immediate possession of the one who believes. In 1 John 5:13 the apostle declared, "I write these things to you who believe in the name of the Son of God so that you may know that you have eternal life" (NIV).

This is God's promise to you and to everyone who believes—children, young people, middle-aged people, and old people. It's for everyone.

Do you know that you have eternal life?

Do you have the assurance of your salvation?

Near the end of his gospel account, the apostle John said that he had written his account of Christ's life "that you may believe that Jesus is the Messiah, the Son of God, and that by believing you may have life in his name" (John 20:31, NIV).

Life in His name. That's the bottom line of everything.

11

TWO WORDS THAT CHANGED EVERYTHING

*Can you think of some-
one whom you could never
imagine as a Christian?
I'm talking about someone
so hardened, so resistant,
and so far gone that he
or she would never follow
Jesus Christ.*

Then again, maybe *you* are such a person (or at least you think you are). Maybe you feel as though you wouldn't qualify to follow Jesus.

I was such a person. I can tell you that it was the last thing I ever planned on doing, but thankfully, God had different plans. My conversion was so unexpected that people didn't believe that Greg Laurie had become a Christian. Yet when I look back on the decision I made and how some of my friends from those earlier days did not make it, I have no regrets whatsoever—not a single one.

Make no mistake about it: conversion *is* instantaneous. While the process of growing and maturing spiritually takes a lifetime, the actual work of conversion can take just seconds. This means that as you read this message, you can, quite literally, change within moments.

I want to tell you the story of a man whose life was dramatically changed after one seemingly short moment of contact with Jesus. It was a moment this man would never, ever forget, not for all eternity.

He was a man who left his career, wealth, and power simply to become a follower of Jesus. It all happened when he came face-to-face with Jesus Christ, who said two words to him: "Follow Me."

His name was Matthew, and this is his story:

Matthew's Story

As Jesus was walking along, he saw a man named Matthew sitting at his tax collector's booth. "Follow me and be my disciple," Jesus said to him. So Matthew got up and followed him.

Later, Matthew invited Jesus and his disciples to his home as dinner guests, along with many tax collectors and other disreputable sinners. But when the Pharisees saw this, they asked his disciples, "Why does your teacher eat with such scum?"

When Jesus heard this, he said, "Healthy people don't need a doctor—sick people do."
(Matthew 9:9–12, NLT)

Looking at the Lord's last comment in the passage above, I'm reminded of how there are two places I don't

Chapter 11: **Two Words That Changed Everything**

like to go: the doctor's office and the dentist's office. (I will only go to the doctor as a last resort and the dentist as a last, *last* resort.) Why am I so reluctant to have myself examined? It's probably because I'm afraid of hearing some bad news. As my wife will tell me, I mistakenly believe that ignorance is bliss.

I heard about a man named Phil who went to the doctor. After a long checkup, his doctor shook his head and said, "Phil, I'm afraid I have some bad news for you. You don't have long to live."

Phil was understandably distraught. "What?? Well, how long do I have?"

"Ten," the doctor said sadly.

"Ten?"

"Ten."

"Ten *what?* Ten months? Ten weeks? Ten days?"

The doctor replied, "Ten, nine, eight, seven . . ."

But back to our story. Tax collectors were looked upon with great hatred by the Jews. For one thing, they collected taxes from their fellow Jews for the Romans, who were the occupying power in Israel at the time. To make matters worse, tax collectors often would skim off the top or charge more than what was required and then personally pocket the overage. It's very possible that Matthew followed this practice as well, but this wasn't the primary reason he was so hated by his countrymen.

Tax collectors like Matthew were regarded as traders and turncoats because they collaborated with the hated Roman overlords. Think of an ambulance-chasing lawyer, a sleazy used-car salesman, and a telemarketer all rolled into one, and you get the idea. Tax collectors barely ranked above plankton on the food chain. It would be like an American collecting intelligence for ISIS. Matthew had aligned himself with the enemies of his own people. It's as though he had gone out of his way to offend his fellow Jews—and God.

We all know people who will do that. They will go far out of their way to offend, to upset, and to put off. Sometimes it's a cry for attention. And sometimes it's because they're running from what they know is right.

Are you running from God right now—perhaps going out of your way to offend Christians and anyone else? Perhaps you are under conviction, and that is why you do what you do. By conviction I mean the Holy Spirit is making you more and more aware of your need for Jesus Christ, and you are fighting and resisting all the way. The ones who put up the biggest fight are often much closer to conversion than those who don't fight at all. As it's been said, when you throw a rock into a pack of dogs, the one that barks the loudest is the one that got hit. Perhaps the reason you are barking the loudest or protesting the most is because you are closer to coming to Jesus than you'd like to let on.

But why had Matthew, also known as Levi, chosen this lifestyle that would alienate and offend so many? We don't know, but we do know this: he was most likely hated by all. All except Jesus.

"Successful" but Unhappy

Matthew's only "friends" would have been other tax collectors.

Maybe you feel as though you are hated. Maybe you are lonely, and you don't even know whether you have any real friends to speak of. Maybe you hate the course your life has taken. You might be into drugs, drinking, partying, or something else. You feel as though life has chewed you up and spit you out. Or maybe you have thought, *If only I could make the big bucks, then I would be happy.*

Musician Dave Matthews makes millions each year from his music and touring, but is he a happy guy? In an interview with *Rolling Stone*, Matthews admitted to being suicidal: "It comes and goes. I don't know that it will ever end. When things inside your head get kind of crazy, and you go, 'OK, let's go through the list of options.' " In the same interview he said, "I like to drink, a lot—I think it's a healthy thing to do. But I've got a family; and I've got other things that impress me more than another drink. . . . I may pause, but I don't think I'll ever stop, because forever is a long time."[1]

The lyrics to one of his songs, "Trouble," perhaps explain why he feels this way:

Here I stand, head bowed for thee
My empty heart begs you, Leave me be!
But I confess you know too well
That I have fallenPray your mercy give to me.[2]

Dave Matthews was a lot like the Matthew of this story. He, too, was a very wealthy and successful man, but he wasn't happy, either. And he had turned his back on the very one who could help him: God. Perhaps something happened that turned him in this direction. Maybe he had been disillusioned by some rabbi or priest. Matthew had been raised to believe, but he turned away, or backslid.

It's amazing how many people will turn away from God at an early age because a minister, priest, or some person who claimed to be a Christian didn't behave as one. People will turn away from Jesus Christ today for the same reason (or excuse). In fact, there are two reasons people don't go to church: (1) they don't know a Christian, or (2) they do know a Christian.

I want you to note, however, that Jesus didn't say to Matthew, "Follow My people." No, He distinctly said, "Follow *Me*." And He says that to you as well. I have been a follower of Jesus for many years, and I can tell you that He has never been a hypocrite or inconsistent in any way. Yes, fellow Christians have disappointed me at times—and I'm sure I've disappointed them as well.

But not Jesus. Jesus always has been who He promised He was to me, and that's why I will follow Him until my last breath.

Matthew would have had a great seat there at his strategically located tax booth. He may have even listened as Jesus taught from a boat. His heart, which undoubtedly had become hardened and bitter by the treatment of others, began to soften. But somehow he couldn't quite bring himself to get up from that tax booth and go to Jesus. He probably was afraid that Jesus would reject him. Maybe he was afraid that Jesus would say, "*You?* Follow *Me?* Do I actually look so desperate that I would want a tax collector to follow Me?"

I can identify with Matthew's reticence to seek out the Lord. When I was a teenager, I would hang out on the streets, just wishing some Christian would come along and talk to me, but they never really did. Thankfully, God could see past my hardened façade and called my name—just like He called Matthew's, and just like He is calling yours.

You may be thinking, *But I'm just not the religious type.* That's good! God isn't looking for the religious type. He is looking for the sinner type. Do you qualify?

Two Words that Changed a Life

One day Jesus saw Matthew and said two words that would forever change Matthew's life:

> As Jesus passed on from there, He saw a man named Matthew sitting at the tax office. And He said to him, "Follow Me." So he arose and followed Him.
> (Matthew 9:9)

The word *saw* in this verse is very suggestive. It means "to gaze intently upon, to stare, to fix one's eyes constantly upon an object." I'm sure that when people walked by Matthew, they would normally either turn their eyes away from him or glare at him with scorn.

In the original language, this word *saw* also means "to look right through." Have you ever had someone look right through you? Or, let me put it another way: Do you have a mother? Jesus intentionally made eye contact with Matthew. And in the eyes of Jesus, Matthew saw many things: holiness and purity, to name a couple. But I'm certain that He also saw love, compassion, and understanding. With their eyes fixed on each other, Jesus said two words that would reverberate through Matthew's soul, words that he never thought he would hear: "Follow Me."

Jesus was choosing, selecting, and calling him out to be His disciple. And Jesus is saying the same thing to you right now.

But what does it mean to "follow Jesus"? Many of us would claim to be His followers. But are we? As 2 Corinthians 13:5 reminds us, "Examine and test and evaluate your own selves to see whether you are holding to your faith and showing the proper fruits of it. Test and prove yourselves [not Christ]. Do you not yourselves realize and know [thoroughly by an ever-increasing experience] that Jesus Christ is in you—unless you are [counterfeits] disapproved on trial and rejected?" (AMP).

But listen to this. The phrase "follow Me" also could be translated "follow *with* Me," meaning companionship and friendship. I love that.

Jesus was saying, "Matthew, I want you to be My friend! Would you follow with Me through life?"

Did you know that Jesus is saying the same to you right now? He wants you to bare your heart to Him, to tell Him your secrets, your fears, your hopes, and your dreams. Jesus said, "You are My friends if you do whatever I command you. No longer do I call you servants, for a servant does not know what his master is doing; but I have called you friends, for all things that I heard from My Father I have made known to you" (John 15:14–15).

Many people think that God is out to ruin their lives. They believe that He is always mad at them. Nothing could be further from the truth. The fact is that God loves you, and His plan for you is good. God says, "For I know the thoughts that I think toward you, says the LORD, thoughts of peace and not of evil, to give you a future and a hope" (Jeremiah 29:11).

Jesus told a well-known story that's become known as the parable of the prodigal son. In effect, this story is a like a snapshot of God, given to us by God Himself. It's kind of like a selfie of the Lord so that we can see what He is really like.

In this story Jesus speaks of a young man who demanded his inheritance from his father and then left home and ended up blowing it all on wild times and immoral living. When he came to his senses and realized that even his father's servants had it better than he did, he decided to go home. His father, who spotted him coming down the road one day, ran out to meet him and threw his arms around him. He welcomed him home and even threw him a party. This father was overjoyed that his prodigal son had come home.

In the same way, when we have sinned against God, He misses us, just as that father missed his wayward son. God wants to be your friend. The question is, do you want to be

His? There are a lot of people running around today who claim to be friends of Jesus. But if you are a true friend of Jesus, then you will obey Him. Remember, Jesus said, "You are My friends if you do whatever I *command* you" (John 15:14, emphasis added). It is not for us to pick and choose which parts of the Bible we like—and then throw out the rest. What God offers is a package deal.

When Jesus said to Matthew, "Follow Me," the word *follow* that He used comes from a Greek word meaning "to walk the same road." It is in the imperative, meaning that Jesus' statement not only was an invitation, but it also was a command. The word is also a verb in the present tense, commanding the beginning of an action and continuing habitually in it. In other words, Jesus was essentially saying, "I command you to follow Me each and every day."

Following Jesus is not something we do only on Sunday. He is not Sunday Jesus but everyday Jesus. He wants to go with you to church, to school, to work, to the movies, as you surf the Net, and wherever you go.

The Bible tells us that Matthew "arose and followed Him" (Matthew 9:9). Luke's gospel adds this detail: "So he [Matthew] left all, rose up, and followed Him" (Luke 5:28).

Matthew, recognizing the incredible privilege being offered, without hesitation stood up and followed Jesus. Do you realize what a privilege it is that Jesus is calling you? As I already mentioned, He called me more than three decades ago as a confused, angry young kid. I wonder where I would be today if I hadn't followed Him.

Chapter 11: Two Words That Changed Everything

You may wonder, *If I follow Jesus, will I have to give up anything?*

Well, yes. And among those things that you give up will be emptiness, loneliness, guilt, regret, and the fear of death. In place of these things, Jesus will give you fulfillment, friendship, forgiveness, and the guarantee of Heaven when you die. It is God's trade-in deal, and it is here for you right now.

It would be like hearing a knock at your front door at home.

"Who is it?" you call out.

"It's Jesus!" a voice replies. "I stand at the door and knock, and if you will hear My voice and open the door, I will come in!"

You swing that door open, and there He stands, Jesus Christ. You quickly invite Him into your living room.

Nervously you ask, "Could I get You something to eat, Jesus?"

"Of course. Thank you," He answers.

You rush into your kitchen, open the door to the refrigerator, and all that's in there is a day-old pizza and a few deviled eggs. Somehow these don't seem appropriate to offer the King of kings. As you're thinking about what to give Jesus to eat, you hear a lot of noise coming from the living room, so you run back in, and there stands Jesus, taking down your pictures from the wall. In the short time you were out of the room, He already has thrown all your furniture onto the front lawn.

Now He is proceeding to tear up your carpet, so you

cry out, "Jesus, with all due respect, what are You doing?"

"A little spring cleaning," He calmly responds.

"But Jesus, this is all my stuff here. And frankly, if I would have known that you were going to get rid of it, I might not have let You in to begin with!"

He ignores your outburst and gives a loud whistle as He gestures to the large moving truck backing up to your driveway. Emblazoned on the sides of it are the words "Father and Son Moving Company."

"Bring it in, boys!" Jesus says, smiling.

Two very large men lay down the most beautiful carpet you have ever seen. Then they begin to put up color-coordinated, lush wall covering. Then new hand-done works of art are hung in the place of your old ones.

"You have really good taste, Jesus!"

"Yes, I do. Don't forget, I did create the heavens and Earth," He answers.

"Good point there, Lord!" you sheepishly respond.

Then gorgeous, handcrafted furniture is carefully laid on your new carpet, and suddenly it dawns on you: Jesus only took away the old things to put something better in their place.

When a person really meets Jesus Christ, he or she cannot leave the old life fast enough. Old habits, standards, and practices are no longer appealing and are gladly left behind.

Far from being depressed about what he left behind, Matthew's heart overflowed with joy. He lost a career but gained a destiny. He lost his material possessions but gained a spiritual fortune. He lost his temporary security but gained eternal life. He gave up all this world had to offer but found Jesus.

You may be like Matthew. Maybe you don't have many friends. Maybe you feel alone and empty. Jesus is looking at you right now and saying, "Follow Me."

He offers you the forgiveness of sin, the hope of Heaven, and peace instead of turmoil. He offers you friendship and companionship instead of loneliness. He offers you Heaven instead of Hell. But you must come to Him—not tomorrow, not next week, month, or year, but now. Jesus is saying to you right now, "Follow Me."

You may think, *God could never change someone like me!*

But He can—and will—right now.

Matthew made a public stand for Jesus Christ. He got right up from that tax booth and followed Jesus.

It would seem to me that Matthew was more of a backslider than an unbeliever. He was raised in the way of the Lord. He knew the Bible but rebelled. But when Jesus spoke to him, he followed.

Have you fallen away from the Lord? Are you living in such a way that if Christ were to return, you wouldn't be ready? God says, "Return, you backsliding children, and I will heal your backslidings" (Jeremiah 3:22).

Some Christian traditions say that after Matthew had served the Lord through his lifetime, he died as a martyr for the Lord. The Bible, however, doesn't tell us what became of him. The last word we have of him in the book of Acts was that he was with the other apostles in an upstairs room, waiting for the coming of the Holy Spirit. There is no record of Matthew ever regretting for one fraction of a second his choice to leave everything and follow Jesus Christ.

Neither will you.

Chapter

FAMOUS

LAST WORDS

For every man or woman on Earth, there will come a last meal, a last breath, and of course, a last statement. And in many ways, what we say in the end is a real insight into what we were in life, what we stood for, and what we lived for. Generally, we die as we have lived.

I read about a man who had been very successful in the restaurant business and had established many restaurants around the United States. When his life was almost over, as he was on his deathbed with his family gathered nearby, he gave his last whisper: "Slice the ham thin!"

On November 30, 1900, the last words of the famous writer Oscar Wilde were, "Either that wallpaper goes, or I do."[1]

Sometimes people know they are giving their last words. Before he was to be hanged for spying on the British, the last words of American patriot Nathan Hale were: "What a pity it is that we can die but once to serve our country."[2]

At other times, people have no idea they're speaking their last words. That apparently was true of William "Buckey" O'Neill, an Arizona lawyer, miner, cowboy, gambler, newspaperman, sheriff, and congressman. He also was one of the most important members of Teddy Roosevelt's Rough Riders during the Spanish-American War. Just prior to the famous charge up Kettle Hill, O'Neill was standing up, smoking a cigarette, and joking with his troops while under withering fire from the ridge. One of his lieutenants shouted a warning to him above the noise.

O'Neill reportedly shouted back his reply, "The Spanish bullet was never moulded [*sic*] that will hit me!"[3]

A short time later, he was hit and killed by a bullet.

Then there were the last words of tenor Richard Versalle, who was performing one night at the Metropolitan Opera, in 1996. Versalle had climbed a ladder for his scene, and after singing the words "Too bad you can only live so long," he suffered a fatal heart attack and fell ten feet to the stage below.[4]

What's more, death is no respecter of persons—even for royalty. On her deathbed, Queen Elizabeth I of England said, "All my possessions for one moment of time."[5] And Princess Diana, following that horrific car accident in a Paris tunnel, was heard to say, "My God, what's happened?"[6]

History tells the story of the renowned atheist Voltaire, who was one of the most aggressive antagonists of Christianity. He once said of Jesus Christ, "Curse the wretch!" He also wrote many things to undermine the church and said, "In twenty years, Christianity will be no more. My single hand shall destroy the edifice it took twelve apostles to rear."[7] But it didn't turn out that way, did it?

The physician waiting up with Voltaire at his death said that he cried out with utter desperation, "I am abandoned by God and man. I will give you half of what I am worth if you will give me six months of life. Then I shall go to Hell and you will go with me, O, Christ! O Jesus Christ!"[8]

What a difference faith makes. The last words of Stephen, who was being stoned to death, were, "Lord Jesus, receive my spirit. . . . Lord, do not charge them with this sin" (Acts 7:59–60).

The great evangelist D. L. Moody, on his deathbed, said, "I see earth receding; Heaven is opening; God is calling me."[9]

The Most Important Last Words Ever

Now let's consider the most famous and important "last words" ever uttered: the words of Jesus as He hung on the cross. I want to focus on one statement in particular, for in it we see what must have been God's most painful moment.

Jesus had been taken to be crucified on the cross, and death by crucifixion was really death by suffocation. It was extremely hard even to breathe, much less speak. Add to this the fact that He had been brutally scourged. The process of scourging was barbaric. The prisoner was tied to a post with his hands over his head, his body taut. The whip had a short, wooden handle with several leather thongs attached, each tipped with sharp pieces of metal or bone. As the whip was brought down on the prisoner, his muscles would be lacerated, veins and arteries would be torn open, and even the kidneys, spleen, or other organs could be exposed and slashed.

Then there was the crucifixion itself, which would cause you to turn away in revulsion at the sight of it. There has never been a movie or painting I've seen that has even come close to depicting what I believe really happened when Jesus died—that is, until Mel Gibson's *The Passion of the Christ*. But I don't know that any artist or filmmaker could ever capture all that happened on that day. Even Gibson has acknowledged that what actually happened to Jesus in His scourging and crucifixion probably was much worse than depicted in his film.

Next to Jesus as He hung on that cross were two criminals who were there for their personal crimes. Jesus, on the other hand, was there for the crimes of all humanity. They were there against their will. Yet Jesus was there because He willingly went. They could not have escaped. But He could have—with just one word to Heaven. They were held to their crosses by nails. Jesus was held to His cross by love.

It is fascinating to see how these three men reacted as they looked death squarely in the face. Initially as Jesus was nailed to the cross, these two men momentarily forgot their personal pain and joined the chorus of the onlookers' voices:

> "He saved others; Himself He cannot save. If He is the King of Israel, let Him now come down from the cross, and we will believe Him. He trusted in God; let Him deliver Him now if He will have Him; for He said, 'I am the Son of God.' "
>
> Even the robbers who were crucified with Him reviled Him with the same thing.
> (Matthew 27:42–44)

How this mockery and unbelief must have pained the tender heart of Jesus. Even there at the cross, they persisted while He was atoning for the very people who were spewing this venom.

In Matthew's account of this event, we read that both thieves joined the crowd in mockery. Luke's gospel, however, reveals a change of heart in one of the felons. Evidently, something significant happened to change the heart of one of these thieves, bringing him to his spiritual senses. Initially, he had joined the chorus of mockery toward Jesus. But then he watched with amazement as Jesus suffered the same crucifixion as he and the other thief had, yet without any complaint, angry protest, or cursing. Then came those unbelievable, unexpected, incomprehensible words of Christ: "Father, forgive them" (Luke 23:34).

How these words must have reverberated through this man's hardened heart! His rebellion, bitterness, and anger that had no doubt driven him all these years melted away, and his heart softened.

While the first word Jesus uttered from the cross was a prayer for His enemies, the second was an answer to prayer, an answer addressed to a single individual. Jesus spoke to him as though he were the only person in the world.

Luke's gospel tells us the believing thief then said, "Lord, remember me when You come into Your kingdom" (23:42), and "Jesus said to him, 'Assuredly, I say to you, today you will be with Me in Paradise' " (verse 43).

In the same way, once you believe in Christ, you can know you are going to Heaven. John said, "These things I have written to you who believe in the name of the Son of God, that you may know that you have eternal life" (1 John 5:13).

Can you imagine the joy that must have filled this man's heart? Talk about being in the right place at the right time! You, too, are in the right place at the right time, even reading the right book at the right time.

The same Jesus who died on that cross and rose from the dead two thousand years ago will forgive you today of all your sins. He is speaking to you right now as though you were the only person in the world.

There is a lot of debate as to who is responsible for the death of Jesus Christ. Was it the Jewish Sanhedrin and the Pharisees? Was it the high priest Caiaphas? Was it the Romans? Or was it Pilate?

I will tell you who is responsible for the crucifixion of Jesus Christ on that cross: *I was!* And so were you. It was *our sins* that put Him there.

Looking ahead to the death of Jesus, the prophet Isaiah wrote these words:

> Yet it was our grief he bore, our sorrows that weighed him down. And we thought his troubles were a punishment from God, for his own sins! But he was wounded and bruised for our sins. He was beaten that we might have peace; he was lashed—and we were healed! (Isaiah 53:4–5, TLB)

Because there was no other way to satisfy the demands of a Holy God, Jesus, who was God, died in our place. The Bible says, "While we were still sinners, Christ died for us" (Romans 5:8). And Paul wrote, "I live by faith in the Son of God, who loved me and gave Himself for me" (Galatians 2:20).

Now the moment comes that Jesus had been dreading. It is here that the tragedy of the Crucifixion reached its horrific climax. In fact, it has been described as "the crucifixion in the Crucifixion":

> Now from the sixth hour until the ninth hour there was darkness over all the land. And about the ninth hour Jesus cried out with a loud voice, saying, "Eli, Eli, lama sabachthani?" that is, "My God, My God, why have You forsaken Me?"
>
> Some of those who stood there, when they heard that, said, "This Man is calling for Elijah!"
>
> Immediately one of them ran and took a sponge, filled it with sour wine and put it on a

reed, and offered it to Him to drink.

The rest said, "Let Him alone; let us see if Elijah will come to save Him."

And Jesus cried out again with a loud voice, and yielded up His spirit.
(Matthew 27:45–50)

Without explanation, the sky turned dark. From the sixth hour (noon) to 3:00 p.m., an ominous darkness fell across the land. The Greek word for *land* in this passage could be translated "earth," possibly indicating the entire world. Some extrabiblical sources suggest that such a universal darkness did occur. A Roman historian mentioned such a darkness. Also, there was a supposed report from Pilate to the Emperor Tiberius that assumed the emperor's knowledge of a certain widespread darkness, even mentioning that it took place from 12:00 p.m. to 3:00 p.m.

The darkness was then pierced by the voice of Jesus: "My God, My God, why have You forsaken Me?" (verse 46). No fiction writer would have his or her hero say words like these. They surprise us, disarm us, and cause us to wonder what He meant. We are looking at something that, in many ways, is impossible for us as humans to fathom.

Martin Luther, after considering these words for days on end, finally gave up trying to wrap his mind around what happened in those moments on the cross. Exasperated, he said, "God forsaken of God! Who can understand it?"[10]

Clearly we are treading on holy ground when we look into such a subject, yet the impact on our lives is so significant that it certainly bears looking into. If we can gain a better understanding of what Jesus actually went through for us and what horrendous pain He experienced, it only gives us a greater appreciation for Him and all He has done for us.

The Worst Moment of All

When Jesus cried out these words, they were not the delusions of a man in pain. His faith was not failing Him. After all, He cried out, "My God, My God . . ."

As Christ hung there, He was bearing the sins of the world. He was dying as a substitute for others and suffering the punishment for their—and my—sins. The very essence of the punishment was the outpouring of God's wrath against sinners. In some mysterious way that we can never fully comprehend, during those awful hours on the cross the Father was pouring out the full measure of His wrath against sin. And the recipient of that wrath was God's own beloved Son! God was punishing Jesus as though He had personally committed every wicked deed of every wicked sinner. And in doing so, He could forgive and treat those redeemed ones as though they had lived Christ's perfect life of righteousness.

The Scriptures clearly teach that this did happen: "For He made Him who knew no sin to be sin for us, that we might become the righteousness of God in Him" (2 Corinthians 5:21). Speaking of God the Father in Isaiah 53:10, the prophet tells us that "It pleased the LORD to bruise Him." We also read that " 'He himself bore our sins' in his body on the cross, so that we might die to sins and live for righteousness; 'by his wounds you have been healed' " (1 Peter 2:24, NIV).

Sin, sin, sin was everywhere around Him at this dreaded moment. We can't begin to fathom what He was going through at this time. All our worst fears about the horrors of Hell—and more—were realized by Him as He received the due penalty of others' wrongdoing.

But the worst of the worst was to be forsaken of God the Father. The physical pains of crucifixion, horrible as they were, were nothing compared to the wrath of the Father being poured out upon Him. This is why, in Gethsemane, "His sweat became like great drops of blood falling down to the ground" (Luke 22:44). This is why He looked ahead to the cross with such horror, because never, not for one moment during His entire earthly ministry, did He ever step outside of intimate fellowship with His Father.

Why, then, did this have to happen?

Because of the unscalable wall between God and man.

God, in all His holiness, could not look at sin because He is "of purer eyes than to behold evil, and cannot look on wickedness" (Habakkuk 1:13). As a result, man, in all his sinfulness, could not look at God. So the Holy Father had to turn His face and pour His wrath upon His own Son.

Understand that for Jesus, this was the greatest sacrifice He could have possibly made. His greatest pain occurred at this moment. To have felt forsaken of God was the necessary consequence of sin. For a man to be forsaken of God is the penalty that naturally and inevitably follows his breaking of his relationship with God.

Jesus was forsaken of God so that I don't have to be. Jesus was forsaken of God for a time so that I might enjoy His presence forever. Jesus was forsaken of God so that I might be forgiven. Jesus entered the darkness so that I might walk in the light. His pain resulted in our gain.

"I Thirst"

After this three-hour ordeal, Jesus gave His fifth statement from the cross—and the first words of a personal nature: "I thirst!" (John 19:28).

First, He prayed for His enemies, then the thief on the cross, then He remembered His mother (see John 19:26) and bore the sins of humanity, and then and only then did He speak of His own needs. Imagine, this was the Creator of the universe making this statement—the One who created water! He could have so easily performed a miracle. After all, He brought water out of rocks in the wilderness. His first earthly miracle during His public ministry was to turn water into wine. He could have simply spoken water into existence.

But it's important to note that Jesus never once performed a miracle for His own benefit or comfort. When tempted by Satan to do this, He refused. Scripture tells us that He was hungry, He grew tired, He wept, and He "was in all points tempted as we are, yet without sin" (Hebrews 4:15). Yes, Jesus was 100 percent God, but He also was a man. He was not a man becoming God (that's impossible), but God who became a man.

Jesus was called "a Man of sorrows" (Isaiah 53:3). What does that mean to you? It means that no matter how great your need, no matter how overwhelming your difficulty, He understands. You can cast "all your care upon Him, for He cares for you" (1 Peter 5:7).

Is your body racked with pain? *So was His.* Have you ever been misunderstood, misjudged, or misrepresented? *So was He.* Have you had your closest friends turn away from you? *So did He.*

Jesus then uttered His sixth statement from the cross: "It is finished!" (John 19:30). The storm had finally passed, the cup had been drained. The Devil had done his worst, and God the Father had bruised Him.

The phrase "It is finished" is translated many ways: "It is made an end of," "It is paid," "It is performed," or "It is accomplished."

What was made an end of? Our sins and the guilt that accompanied them.

What was paid? The price of redemption.

What was performed? The righteous requirements of the law.

What was accomplished? The work the Father had given Him to do.

Three days later, Jesus Christ came out of His tomb, rising from the dead. He is alive and here right now, wanting to come into your life.

We see three things as we look at the Cross.

1. WE SEE THAT IT'S A DESCRIPTION OF THE DEPTH OF MAN'S SIN

It's been said that you can tell the depth of a well by how much rope is lowered. So don't blame the people of that day for putting Jesus on that cross. You and I are just as guilty. It wasn't the Roman soldiers who put Him on that cross; it was your sins and my sins that made it necessary for Him to die this torturous and humiliating death.

2. WE SEE THE OVERWHELMING LOVE OF GOD

If ever you are tempted to doubt God's love for you, just take a long look at the cross that He hung on for you. Romans 5:8 tells us, "But God demonstrates His own love toward us, in that while we were still sinners, Christ died for us."

3. WE SEE THAT THE CROSS IS THE ONLY WAY OF SALVATION

Jesus said, "I am the way, the truth, and the life. No one comes to the Father except through Me" (John 14:6). If there had been any other way to save you, He would have found it. If living a good, moral life would save you, then Jesus never would have died. But He *did* die. Because there was—and is—no other way.

HOW TO

CHANGE YOUR LIFE

Without question, God loves you deeply and wants to reveal the personal, custom-made plan that He has just for you. He wants to flood your life with peace, joy, and purpose. Ultimately, He wants to spend all eternity with you in a place that exceeds your wildest dreams—a place called Heaven.

God says, "For I know the thoughts that I think toward you . . . thoughts of peace and not of evil, to give you a future and a hope" (Jeremiah 29:11).

But just as surely as there is a loving God who cares for you, there is a hateful Devil who wants to destroy you. He is like "a roaring lion, seeking whom he may devour" (1 Peter 5:8). Jesus, in speaking of Satan, said that he comes "to steal, and to kill, and to destroy" (John 10:10).

That pretty much sums up Satan's agenda: *steal, kill, and destroy.*

On the other hand, Jesus comes "that [we] may have life, and that [we] may have it more abundantly" (John 10:10).

In the Scriptures we find the story of a man who had been completely taken over by the power of the Devil. He was a tortured, suicidal, miserable, lonely shell of a man in an absolutely hopeless situation.

This basically shows us the package deal Satan has in store for every person in his grip. First and foremost, he wants to keep you from coming to Jesus Christ. He may entice you with all the glitz and glamour this world has to offer. It may be greed for the acquisition of things. It may be sexual lust. But once he has you where he wants you, he'll chew you up and spit you out.

Judas Iscariot is the classic example. It's hard to believe, but those thirty pieces of silver offered by the religious leaders looked pretty appealing to him. Yet once the Devil had what he wanted, Judas was cast aside like yesterday's garbage.

The stuff this world offers us can look so cool and so appealing.

Madonna is someone who has "been there, done that." She has said, "Take it from me. I went down the road of 'be all you can be, realize your dreams,' and I'm telling you that fame and fortune are not what they're cracked up to be."[1]

The world's idea of fulfillment is a complete rip-off, and the result is frightening.

The story before us illustrates these points. And in this story, we see three forces at work: Satan, culture, and Christ. We will see what Satan did, what culture offered, and then what Jesus Christ did.

Here is how Matthew captures that dramatic story.

The First Force at Work: Satan

When He had come to the other side, to the country of the Gergesenes, there met Him two demon-possessed men, coming out of the tombs, exceedingly fierce, so that no one could pass that way. And suddenly they cried out, saying, "What have we to do with You, Jesus, You Son of God? Have You come here to torment us before the time?"

Now a good way off from them there was a herd of many swine feeding. So the demons begged Him, saying, "If You cast us out, permit us to go away into the herd of swine."

And He said to them, "Go." So when they had come out, they went into the herd of swine. And suddenly the whole herd of swine ran violently down the steep place into the sea, and perished in the water.

(Matthew 8:28–32)

As our story begins, we find two pathetic, demented men. In Luke's account of this story, he zeroes in on one of these men in particular. He seemed to be the more extreme of the two: "And when He stepped out on the land, there met Him a certain man from the city who had demons for a long time. And he wore no clothes, nor did he live in a house but in the tombs" (Luke 8:27). In addition to this, he would beat and bruise himself as well as cut himself with sharp rocks. He was so strong that when he was put in chains, he broke them.

So here was quite a creepy scenario: a frightening, evil man with superhuman strength, who hung out at the graveyard. No doubt local people gave this place a wide berth, especially at night. Superstitious people would have said this was a place for ghosts and goblins. This man who lived in the tombs certainly was a dangerous and frightening man, but underneath that dark exterior was a truly tortured soul. And, as I mentioned earlier, he is a picture of Satan's ultimate goal—the finished product.

What steps led to this state we can only imagine. But here we see the package deal of sin, Satan, and death, all intertwined together. What a dark and depressing situation. Sin truly is a living death, and the unbeliever is spiritually "dead in trespasses and sins" (Ephesians 2:1). The Bible says, "But she who lives in pleasure is dead while she lives" (1 Timothy 5:6).

Nevertheless, this is a story with a happy ending. Why?

Because Jesus came into this poor, tortured man's life and made him into an altogether different kind of person.

When Jesus showed up at this place seeking out these men, Satan reacted with force: "They began screaming at him, 'Why are you interfering with us, Son of God? Have you come here to torture us before God's appointed time?'" (Matthew 8:29, NLT). The power of Satan was so entwined with this man that most would not have been able to see the hurting person deep inside, but only the crazed, suicidal maniac roaming the graveyard. Yet in this cry, Jesus must have also heard a cry for help.

Perhaps that describes you right now. Underneath all of your talk and bravado and arguments against God, you secretly long for His help and for some peace and purpose in your life. Underneath an outward show of confidence, you may be lonely and afraid.

This man may not have been doing many right or wise things, but on that day he did. He realized that he did not have power and that he was trapped beyond human hope by the Enemy. So he cried out to Jesus. And Jesus came to him.

The only thing stronger than the power of Satan is the power of Jesus.

The demons possessing this man screamed out a bizarre question: "What have we to do with You, Jesus, You Son of God? Have You come here to torment us before the time?"

The apostle James tells us, "You believe that there is one God. You do well. Even the demons believe—and tremble!" (James 2:19). It may surprise you to know that the demons, and the Devil himself, are neither atheists nor agnostics. They believe in the existence of God. They believe in the deity of Jesus Christ. They believe that the Bible is the very

Word of God. They believe Jesus is coming back again. In fact, you could say that (in a very limited sense) demons and the Devil are quite orthodox in their beliefs. But they are *not* followers of Christ.

I remember as a very young Christian hearing someone say, "Let's pray for Satan's conversion!" Even as a newly minted follower of Jesus, I thought this was ridiculous. It's not going to happen! The point in James's words is simply this: It's not enough to simply believe in God. It's not enough to believe that Jesus is the Son of God. It's not enough to believe that the Bible is the Word of God. *You must personally choose to follow Jesus.*

In Luke's account of this story, we read that Jesus asked, "What is your name?" (Luke 8:30).

Luke tells us the man answered, " 'Legion,' because many demons had entered him" (verse 30). This man was so wrapped up in demonic powers that he couldn't even answer for himself. A Roman legion consisted of six thousand soldiers, which means this man was possessed by perhaps hundreds, even thousands, of demons.

Somewhere along the line, these men had opened themselves up to satanic invasion. They played around with sin, and therefore sin was playing around with them. They had lost everything—their homes, their families, their friends, their sanity, and even their will. They were completely under the power of the Devil.

We must remember this when we start playing games with sin. Satan will dangle what he must in front of you to get you to take the bait.

There are many who open the door to the supernatural through their use of drugs, as there is a definite link between drugs and the occult. The Bible warns of the sin of sorcery, and in fact, the word *sorcery* comes from the Greek word *pharmakeia*, the same word from which our English word *pharmacy* is derived. The biblical definition of sorcery has to do with the illicit use of drugs. When people begin to use drugs, whether it's marijuana (which really is a gateway drug to cocaine and heroin) or any other mind-controlling substance, it opens them up to the spiritual realm.

Marijuana may be in widespread use and even legalized in some of our states. But that only means there will be a wider door for the occult to gain a foothold in our communities.

Dabbling in black magic, witchcraft, Ouija boards, or astrology also can open the door. The Bible tells us that "those who practice such things will not inherit the kingdom of God" (Galatians 5:21).

I did drugs for a couple of years. I already had been drinking and into the party scene and thought drugs finally would be the thing that would fill some of those big, empty places in my life. But drugs only made my problems worse and made that void in my heart seem even deeper and wider. That huge emptiness in my life only could be filled by God Himself.

The Second Force at Work: Culture

As I pointed out earlier, we see three forces at work in this story: Satan, culture, and Christ. We've already seen what Satan did with these men. So what did culture do for them?

It chained them up.

We have a wave of violent crime sweeping across our country, with vicious gangs growing and spreading in many communities. Law enforcement is often understaffed and underpaid. Many of our courts and judges give out lenient sentences. And sadly, the family is continuing to fall apart at an unprecedented rate. Meanwhile, back in our schools, situational ethics are taught, asserting there really is no such thing as absolute values, right or wrong, black or white, but only shades of gray. What is a society to do? Like those in Jesus' day, we just lock people up.

According to an article in *The Washington Post*, America's prison population today stands at more than 2.4 million people, which has "more than *quadrupled* since 1980." It basically means that "one out of every one hundred American adults is behind bars" today.[2]

With all of their wonderful scientific achievements, society and culture still cannot cope with the problems caused by Satan and sin.

No one could help these demon-possessed men. Their situation was absolutely hopeless. But what the chains could not do, Jesus did with one word.

The Third Force at Work: Jesus Christ

What did Jesus do for these men? He sought them out in their spooky little graveyard and offered them hope. And apparently, these demons preferred inhabiting something instead of nothing, so Jesus conceded to their request and sent them into a herd of pigs. The pigs all went over the cliff in madness. You might say that it was the first recorded mention of deviled ham.

Luke's account of this story tells us what happened to this man who was delivered: "People rushed out to see what had happened. A crowd soon gathered around Jesus, and they saw the man who had been freed from the demons. He was sitting at Jesus' feet, fully clothed and perfectly sane, and they were all afraid" (8:35, NLT).

What a change!

If you want proof of the existence of God, then just look at the changes He has made in the lives of people you know who have given their lives to Jesus Christ.

Not long ago I met a man from the Czech Republic who gave me his firsthand story of how Christ had changed his life:

I grew up in the Czech Republic and in a family where my father was an alcoholic. My first drunkenness occurred when I was three years old, when my father left me in a room with glasses of liquor while he was partying with another guy. They took me to a hospital and found that I had been drunk for fifty hours and had almost died. I grew up in the communist system. It gave me a rough, hard, and angry attitude. Soon I was known as a fistfighter and an angry man. As I got older, I became even more violent. I went into the military. I spent a short time in prison for violence, alcoholism, and drunkenness.

He then explained that he relocated to the United States and moved in with a girl. He went on to say,

I continued my spiral into alcohol and all the rest of it. On one occasion, my life was spinning down into the bottomless pit. I lost fifty pounds and was ready to commit suicide. I was staring at a gun I was pointing in my mouth. I didn't have any resolve to live. My whole life was one big emptiness, only existing, just a waste of time.

Here was this man—hopeless, alcoholic, violent, and suicidal. And what happened? He continued,

At that time, my neighbor in Mission Viejo and her friends invited me to the Harvest Crusade in 1994. After the music and the message, I knew the Lord was knocking, was on my heart, and wanted me to give up being in control of my life. I got up, walked down to the platform, and asked the Lord to take me out of this garbage and mess, and if He did that, I would do anything He asked. God's Spirit surrounded me and began to melt all of the pain and hurts that I had all of those years, and God's Word started to work in a miraculous way in my life.

He started going to church and learning the Word of God, and now he has gone back to his homeland, has started a church, and is preaching the gospel. What this world can't do, Jesus Christ can.

Jesus delivered the suicidal, tormented, demon-possessed man. So how did the people react? Amazingly, they were afraid. The demonstration of the power of God frightened them. They should have been rejoicing and praising God, but instead they became very anxious and uncomfortable. They couldn't understand or process what had just happened, and rather than seeking to learn more about it, they wanted to push it away and hide it from their sight.

You would have thought they would have asked Jesus to stay with them and perhaps heal some more people or teach them about this power that could transform lives. But they did the very opposite: "Then the whole multitude of the surrounding region of the Gadarenes asked Him to depart from them, for they were seized with great fear" (Luke 8:37).

The owners of the swine were angry at Jesus. For some people, after all, Jesus is bad for business. Apparently they felt that something might be required of them. In their case it was an economic loss. So they decided it would be best for Jesus to go away. Hogs were big business on this side of the lake. Clearly, if Jesus stuck around, it might hurt the economy. Two thousand hogs is a lot of bacon, and they were at the bottom of the lake.

But the fact that Jesus was bad for business wasn't

the only reason these residents wanted Jesus to go away. More than that, they must have wondered, *If He did that for this one man, would He do the same to us?* Sometimes the prospect of change can seem frightening. It's much more comfortable to live in the same old rut, doing the same old stuff—even if you're bored or miserable.

Then there was their own guilt. The presence of Jesus Christ always will awaken that. They could see in His eyes that He knew everything about them and read them like an open book. Just as He cast the demons out of the men and into the pigs, so He seemed able to look through them and see their deepest thoughts. They felt themselves withering in His presence and were highly nervous about what He might say or do.

What if He wanted to bring change into their lives?

What if He turned things upside down (or right side up)?

The prospect was too unsettling. It would be much easier if He just went away.

It's important to note, however, that before conversion, there must first come the conviction of sin. Guilt comes before repentance because it shows us our desperate need. But remember this: the very One who causes us to experience that guilt also can remove it—forever.

These people told Jesus to go away. And He did.

Will you do the same? Really, when you get down to it, this sums up the reaction of all humanity to Jesus Christ. It's either "Away with Him!" or "Follow Him." In the final analysis, each of us belongs to one of those groups.

You might protest that and say, "I admit that I haven't made a commitment to Christ or said, 'I want to be with Him,' but I've never said, 'Away with Him!' either. I simply haven't decided yet."

But to not be for Jesus *is* to be against Him. Either we pray for Him to go away, or we pray to ask Him into our lives. Which is it for you?

What are some ways people say, "Away with Him"?

Some reject Jesus out of fear. Perhaps there was a time when they were sitting in church and God began to work on their hearts. They realized this was both true and exactly what they needed. A little bit of hope and a little bit of joy began to bubble up as they edged nearer to God. Yet because of their fear of what their friends would think, or fear of mockery, they resisted and shook off the influence. They vowed not to go back to church. In essence they said, "Away with Jesus!"

Others reject Jesus out of selfishness. God has clearly shown us in His Word what is right and wrong, but they have decided to do what they want to do. They will continue in that sexual relationship with someone they aren't married to. They will continue partying their lives away. They will continue with that drug or alcohol use. Though God has spoken to their hearts through conscience, friends, and, of course, His Word, they are in essence saying, "Away with Jesus!"

Others reject Jesus because of busyness. This isn't as blatant as deliberately breaking His commandments. These are just people who get so wrapped up with the concerns and activities of life—work, family, responsibilities, and hobbies—that there isn't any room for Jesus. They don't deliberately push Him away. They're just too preoccupied and busy to care much about Him.

Which is it for you? Is it "Away with Jesus!" or "Lord, come into my heart"?

Do you know what Jesus did when they told Him to go away?

He left. Matthew tells us, "Then the entire town came out to meet Jesus, but they begged him to go away and leave them alone. Jesus climbed into a boat and went back across the lake to his own town" (8:34–9:1, NLT).

I can't help wondering what it was like in that neighborhood after they sent Jesus away. Do you suppose that people felt a little empty? A little lonely? A little restless? Do you think they might have experienced some regret as they reflected on what had happened in their midst?

The fact is that Jesus is a gentleman. He will not force His way into your life. He says, "Behold, I stand at the door and knock" (Revelation 3:20). He doesn't say, "Open up, or I'll jimmy the lock and kick the door in!"

There never has been a better time for you to get right with God than now. The Bible says, "Now is the day of salvation" (2 Corinthians 6:2), and "Seek the LORD while He may be found, call upon Him while He is near" (Isaiah 55:6).

You may never have another opportunity like this one.

14

THE GOD WHO
LOVES AND FORGIVES

Years ago I had a German shepherd named Irlo. (He came prenamed.) He was the best dog I've ever owned. I loved that dog!

One night I was taking him out for a walk when a cat ran by. I don't want to say that I encouraged my dog to chase the cat. Let's just say that I didn't exactly *discourage* him. In fact, I may have said, "Get 'em, Irlo!"

Irlo took off like a shot, and suddenly the cat stopped in the middle of the street. I thought to myself, *What kind of cat is this?*

The cat lifted up its tail, and I heard a sound. *Psshhew.* Then I noticed that the cat had a white stripe down its back—and that it wasn't a cat at all. It was a skunk, and it had just scored a direct hit on Irlo's face. Irlo did an instant 180 and started running back toward me. In the meantime, I was running from Irlo because I wanted to get back to the house before he did. I also remembered that I'd left the front door open—which meant that if he got there before me, he would run inside and stink up the whole house.

I ran as fast as I could, but Irlo ran faster, passed me, and sped like a rocket through the open door. Of course he was in a frenzy and ran through the whole house, trying to escape the smell.

Finally I corralled him and got him into the backyard. It woke up my wife—who has a supersonic nose at the best of times—out of a dead sleep.

It took a long time to remove the essence of skunk from Irlo and from our house.

That whole incident reminds me a little of guilt. Once you experience it, it's not easy to get rid of. Maybe you're dealing with a heavy load of guilt right now. You've tried to talk yourself out of it. You've tried to drown it out with activity and noise. You've sought to minimize it. You've told yourself that it isn't real. You've said, "I don't need to concern myself with this."

But it *is* real, and you know it.

What's more, it's always there, hanging over you like a cloud.

Contrary to what people in our contemporary culture will tell you, guilt isn't always a bad thing. Guilt is a symptom of a deeper problem.

And the deeper problem is sin.

You feel guilty because you have sinned, and that means your conscience is working. The fact is that sometimes you have to feel bad before you can feel good. Jesus said, "Blessed are those who mourn, for they shall be comforted" (Matthew 5:4). First you have to see your real condition. Your conscience is telling you that something isn't right.

Years ago we used to have a smoke alarm in our ceiling in the kitchen. This was the most overly sensitive smoke alarm I have ever seen. My wife would cook up a scrambled egg, and the alarm would go off. If you put a piece of bread in the toaster, the alarm would go off. I'd have to pull the broom out of the closet and push the little button. It was ridiculous. You couldn't cook anything in the kitchen because of this overly sensitive smoke alarm. One day it went off, and I couldn't take any more. I climbed up on a stool, ripped it out of the ceiling, and that was the end of it.

Let me counsel you here: Don't do that to your heart. If your heart is working, if your conscience is functional, and if you're feeling bad about some things you have said or done, that may be a good indication. But like the red light that blinks on the instrument panel of your car when something's wrong with your engine, this may be something you need to take care of.

Here's the bottom line. You shouldn't feel like the Lone Ranger, because every one of us has sinned. What does it mean to sin? It means to cross a line. The Bible speaks of our being "dead in trespasses and sins" (Ephesians 2:1).

Maybe at some point you walked through a park and saw a little sign that said No Trespassing, but you ignored the sign and went over the line. That's what it means to sin. You cross a line—God's line.

God has given us absolute standards for right and wrong, and they're called the Ten Commandments. Sometimes I will hear people say, "I live by the Ten Commandments. That's all the religion I need."

The fact is, however, that even if you could name them (and most people can't), you couldn't live by them. No one can. No one lives by the Ten Commandments. We've all broken them, we've all crossed the line, and we've all fallen short of God's standard—which is perfection. The Bible says, "For there is no difference; for all have sinned and fall short of the glory of God" (Romans 3:22–23).

We all have sinned. We all have guilt. That's the bad news. But here's the good news. No matter what sin you have committed, God can forgive it and remove it from you forever. You can become a whole new person on the inside.

Lost at Sea

Have you ever lost anything in the ocean when you were swimming or surfing? Maybe a ring or a watch or sunglasses? You can pretty much say good-bye to that item because most likely you will never see it again.

Years ago I went scuba diving. I was cruising along about fifteen feet down, looking at the sea about thirty feet below me. Then I came to a ledge of some kind, and the sea floor dropped out of sight. Though the water was crystal clear, I could no longer see the bottom. I was swimming over a dark void.

Even though I was still only fifteen feet underwater, I had a funny feeling in my stomach. The depths were freaking me out a little, and I had to go back over to the ledge where I could see the bottom again.

If I were to drop something over that ledge in the sea, it would fall a long, long way down. I would never, ever see it again.

That's what God will do with our sins. The Bible says that God will "hurl all our iniquities into the depths of the sea" (Micah 7:19, NIV). God Himself says, "Their sins and their lawless deeds I will remember no more" (Hebrews 10:17).

You see, this really is good news. God not only will forgive your sin, but He also will deliberately choose to forget your sin.

Two Men, Two Responses to Jesus

The Bible tells the story of two thieves on two crosses, crucified on the same day that Jesus was, and hanging on each side of Him. The word translated "thief" in the New Testament is a much more intense word than our word. We're not talking about petty shoplifters here. These guys probably were murderers and insurrectionists who had revolted against Roman tyranny. We might call them terrorists today.

So there they were that day, two men hanging on crosses for their own sins, and Jesus hanging on a cross for the sins of others. The people down below the cross, looking on, began to mock Christ. They said, "He saved others; let him save himself if he is God's Messiah, the Chosen One" (Luke 23:35, NIV). It wasn't long before the two men on the other crosses joined in the mockery.

But then Jesus said something that must have blown the mind of one of those thieves. He said, "Father, forgive them, for they do not know what they do" (verse 34).

At some point, one of the men crucified next to Jesus looked right at Him and said, "Lord, remember me when You come into Your kingdom" (verse 42).

He believed right on the spot, and Jesus said to him, "Assuredly, I say to you, today you will be with Me in Paradise" (verse 43).

Becoming a Christian can happen in an instant. It doesn't take a year. It doesn't take a month. It doesn't take a week. It can happen in a heartbeat. Maybe it has already happened to you. God has touched your heart with the Good News of the gospel, and you have said, "I believe this. I understand that Jesus loves me and that He came to die on the cross for me."

Just that quickly, you cross over from death to life (see John 5:24).

That felon on the cross had been hopeless up to that point. But suddenly, at the very worst of times, he found hope. In spite of all of the agony of the moment, can you imagine how his heart must have leaped with joy? Jesus had just said to him, "Today *you* will be with *Me* in *Paradise*" (emphasis added).

Have You Lost Hope?

We all remember hearing about the tragic suicide of comedian and actor Robin Williams. This was a man who lost hope and was so despondent—in spite of family, fame, and fortune—that he ended his own life. Have you lost hope? Maybe at some point you have even thought about—or attempted—suicide. It has been said that man can live forty days without food, three days without water, about eight minutes without air, but only one second without hope. *Jesus Christ can give you hope right now, just as He gave it to that thief on the cross two thousand years ago.*

The man being executed on the cross had what we might call a deathbed conversation with Jesus. I've spoken to people who have told me, "I'll wait until my deathbed to believe in Jesus. Until then, I'll party and have fun and break all the rules. Then, when I'm ten minutes away from death, I'll believe."

But what makes them think they will have the luxury of a deathbed conversion? Sometimes death comes without warning. The Bible says, "It is appointed for men to die once, but after this the judgment" (Hebrews 9:27).

We often hold our Harvest Crusades in baseball stadiums. I heard the story about two guys who were longtime friends and huge baseball fans. John and Josh talked and texted often, and it always was about baseball. Somewhere along the line, they made a deal with one another: Whoever died first would somehow find a way to tell the living one whether or not there was baseball in Heaven.

When John passed away, his friend Josh waited and waited to hear a word from the other side. After about a week, he heard John's voice.

"I'm here in Heaven, Josh, and it's fantastic!"

"You've got to answer the question," Josh replied. "Is there baseball in Heaven?"

John said, "I've got some good news and bad news about that, Josh."

"Oh yeah? What's the good news?"

"The good news is there is baseball in Heaven."

"Well, that's great to hear," Josh replied. "But what's the bad news?"

"You are pitching Friday night."

Yes, that's a joke. But it illustrates how life can end unexpectedly. This could very well be your last opportunity to get right with God.

The Man Who Hunted Christians

Setting aside those two fictional baseball fans, I want to talk about someone who might be regarded as a very evil man. He murdered innocent people—men and women. He tortured others. He caused many to live in fear, always looking over their shoulders. He wasn't a hit man for La Cosa Nostra, but in many ways he was just as bad.

This man was known as Saul, and he came from the city of Tarsus, in what is today southern Turkey, but he moved to Israel. In his era, he was a member of an elite religious group called the Sanhedrin—something like the Supreme Court of their day. They made rulings that affected the whole nation. Saul made it his business—with the blessing of Israel's religious leaders—to hunt down followers of Jesus and put them to death.

Difficult as it may be to comprehend, this sort of bloody persecution against believers in Jesus continues to this day. The terrorist organization ISIS has been hunting down Christians throughout a large swath of Syria and Iraq—torturing them, killing them, burying whole families alive, and sometimes even crucifying them. When these terrorists find the home of a believer, they spray paint the letter *N* on that home in Arabic. The *N* stands for "Nazarene" because Christians follow the Nazarene.

Two millennia ago, it was Saul hunting down the followers of the Nazarene. One day these anti-Christian activists hauled a brave young man named Stephen in front of Saul and the rest of the Sanhedrin. The Bible says, "As all those who sat on the High Council looked at Stephen, they found they couldn't take their eyes off him—his face was like the face of an angel!" (Acts 6:15, MSG).

When they gave Stephen a chance to speak, he declared the gospel of Jesus without any fear or shame. As he spoke, these leaders became more and more angry. They weren't just annoyed or nettled. They were furious. In fact, they became so enraged that they put their fingers in their ears and started screaming. (You know your message isn't going over very well when people start doing that.)

Even so, Stephen kept right on speaking. The men on the council rushed at him and dragged him out into the street to stone him to death. As the rocks were hurtled at Stephen's young body, he cried out, "Lord, don't charge them with this sin!" (Acts 7:60, NLT). It sounds just like

Jesus on the cross when He said, "Father, forgive them, for they know not what they do."

Saul was there, approved of this brutal execution, and stood guard over the coats of those who were throwing the stones.

Stephen was a young man who loved life, but he wasn't afraid to die. He knew that as a believer, death wasn't the end for him but the beginning of a new life in Heaven.

Are you afraid to die? Death will come for every one of us. As someone has said, the statistics on death are pretty impressive: one out of every one person will die.

That doesn't mean that Christians walk around with some kind of a death wish. The fact is that I don't think anyone loves life more than a Christian. We don't need drugs or alcohol to make life fulfilling because we have a relationship with the living God Himself. Nevertheless, when the day comes for us to die, we will be ready. As the apostle Paul said (and by the way, Saul of Tarsus *became* the apostle Paul), "For to me, to live is Christ and to die is gain" (Philippians 1:21, NIV).

That is the hope of the follower of Jesus Christ. Only those who are prepared to die are really ready to live.

After watching Stephen die so courageously for Jesus, Saul went on a rampage, hunting down Christians. Why was he in such a frenzy? I think it was because God's Holy Spirit already was working on him, seeking to draw him to Jesus. Sometimes the people who argue the most and the loudest may be closer to the kingdom of God than those who are passive and nice about it.

When you read the account in the Bible, you don't see this young man Stephen reaching great numbers of people for Jesus in his short life. But he did reach one. He reached Saul of Tarsus, who later *became* the apostle Paul. Not a bad life's work.

"Who Are You, Lord?"

Maybe a Christian in your life has attracted your attention. There is something about this person's life that has you thinking.

My friend Lee Strobel used to be the legal editor for the *Chicago Tribune*. When his wife became a Christian, it really made him angry. He was an atheist, and having a Christian wife didn't fit in with his lifestyle. Being a legal editor and a very intelligent man, he decided that he would take a weekend and disprove his wife's newfound faith.

So he threw himself into the research, but it didn't turn out the way he had expected. He ended up concluding that everything his wife believed was true and that Jesus Christ was truly the Lord and the Son of God. Lee committed his life to Christ and has become one of the leading apologists in the church today.

Saul was burning with hatred for believers. In Acts 9:1 we read that he was "still breathing out murderous threats against the Lord's disciples" (NIV). In another translation, it says he was "out for the kill. He went to the Chief Priest and got arrest warrants to take to the meeting places in Damascus so that if he found anyone there belonging to the Way, whether men or women, he could arrest them and bring them to Jerusalem" (Acts 9:1–2, MSG).

That was when something very dramatic and completely unexpected happened to this man who was so full of hate and venom:

> As he neared Damascus on his journey, suddenly a light from heaven flashed around him. He fell to the ground and heard a voice say to him, "Saul, Saul, why do you persecute me?"
>
> "Who are you, Lord?" Saul asked.
>
> "I am Jesus, whom you are persecuting," he replied.
>
> (Acts 9:3–5, NIV)

Saul had been driven by hate. This reminds me of another friend of mine, Raul Ries, a Vietnam veteran who came back from the war full of anger. One night he decided that he was going to kill his wife and his sons. He was waiting at home for them with a loaded shotgun. As he was sitting there in his living room, he turned on the television and saw some guy talking about the love of God. That man's name, by the way, was Pastor Chuck Smith. Raul Ries, who only moments before had been filled with murder, bitterness, and hatred, got down on his knees and asked God to forgive him of his sins. Now Raul is a pastor of a church, and God has used him all around the world.

The point is that no one is beyond the reach of God—not Greg Laurie, not Lee Strobel, not Raul Reis, not Saul of Tarsus, and not you, either.

Later on, when the newly converted Saul began talking to people about Jesus, no one could believe it. "*Is that Saul? Isn't that the Christian killer? And he's talking about faith in Jesus? No way!*"

That would be like hearing that Richard Dawkins, one of today's leading spokespersons for atheists, had become a Christian and had written a book about his faith in Christ.

You would say, "Dawkins? A Christian? I can't believe it!"

It would be like hearing that Howard Stern had turned his radio program into a Bible study show or that Bill Maher had become an evangelist, with Lady Gaga leading worship and Ozzy Osbourne doing follow-up. It sounds silly. It sounds incomprehensible. But nothing is impossible with God. If God could change Saul of Tarsus, He can change *anyone*.

Religion . . . or a Relationship?

Saul thought he was on a mission for God when he found out that he had actually been fighting with God.

He heard that voice saying, "Saul, Saul, why are you persecuting Me?"

"Who are You, Lord?" he asked. (And I can just imagine him saying to himself, "Don't say Jesus! Please, don't say Jesus!")

But then the voice said, "I am Jesus . . ." (Acts 9:4-5).

And with that, this man's entire world turned upside down. He was actually opposing the very God he thought he had been serving. Do you know what Paul's problem was? *His religion had kept him from God.* And when it's all said and done, I think religion probably will send more people to Hell than all of the other sins out there.

What is religion? Religion is man's attempt to reach God—through rituals, through traditions, through things that we do or practice. But here is the difference between a religion and a relationship with God: In a religion, man is reaching out to God. In Christianity, God is reaching down to man through Christ.

That's a very big difference. Religion says *do.* Do this, and you will reach nirvana. Do this, and you will find inner peace. Do this other thing, and you might get to Heaven. In contrast, Christianity says *done.* Your salvation has been paid in full at the Cross by Jesus Christ because of His shed blood. It's done! Jesus accomplished it for us.

Religion, for whatever good it might do, won't get you to Heaven. The conventional wisdom, of course, is that good people go to Heaven and bad people go to Hell. Let me correct that, because it isn't true. In fact, in many cases the reverse might be true. The fact of the matter is that there will be "good people" who will go to Hell, and there will be "bad people" who will go to Heaven.

Please hear me on this: If those "good people" think they're so good that they don't need Jesus Christ, they never will get to Heaven. I don't care who you are. You're not good enough. You still fall short of God's standards. But if those "bad people" admit their sin and turn from it, Jesus Christ will forgive them, just like He forgave the thief on the cross, just like He forgave Saul of Tarsus, just like

He forgave Greg Laurie, and just like He will forgive you—if you turn to Him in faith right now.

I would imagine there will be at least three surprises when we get to Heaven: (1) some of the people we thought would be there won't be there, (2) some of the people we never thought would be there will be there, and (3) *you* will be there.

Saul's life was dramatically, irreversibly changed. He became such a different man that he even changed his name to Paul. He got rid of the crushing guilt that plagued him, and he became a new man with a new purpose.

Have you heard the voice of God speak to you recently? When you do, it probably won't be audible. It will be more like someone tugging on your heart, deep down inside you. Jesus said, "Here I am! I stand at the door and knock. If anyone hears my voice and opens the door, I will come in and eat with that person, and they with me" (Revelation 3:20, NIV). Have you heard His voice?

In Acts 9, when Saul heard the voice from Heaven, the people with him heard a noise but didn't recognize it as a voice. But Saul knew! I've been doing evangelistic crusades in large stadiums and arenas around the world for twenty-five years now. And I know very well that there is nothing I can say or do to make you believe in Jesus. All I can do is tell you the truth and pray that God's Holy Spirit will open your heart to the truth of my words.

When I get a call on my cell phone, I look down to see whose name is on the screen. If it says "Cathe Laurie," I take the call. That's my wife, and if I possibly can, I always will answer it. And Cathe answers my calls, too (if the battery isn't dead, and if she doesn't have the ringer turned off).

But what if you looked down at your phone and saw that you had a call from Jesus Christ? You're thinking, *Whoa! How did He get my number?* The truth is that He has always had your number. He has it written across the palm of His hand.

If you received such a call from Jesus, you'd have a decision to make. You could accept the call or decline it. You could answer the call or ignore it. You could say yes to Him or no. It really is an either-or proposition.

Jesus never said, "Admire Me," or "Respect Me," or "Have a high regard for Me."

He said, "Follow Me."

And He still does.

15

SEE YOU

IN THE MORNING

The advent of GPS devices couldn't have come too soon for me. I have always been navigation-ally challenged. In other words, I get lost all the time. Now I can punch in the address on my GPS device and start driving. It even talks to me! It will say, "Turn right at the next off-ramp."

My GPS actually criticizes me if I miss a turn. It will say, "So why didn't you turn at the last off-ramp? I *told* you to turn right at the next off-ramp!" (I'm going to have to go into the settings of the device and figure out how to turn off the nag utility so it will stop doing that.)

We talk as though we're so amazing and advanced for inventing a Global Positioning System. But God has been way ahead of us on that from the beginning of Creation. Think about the GPS system—or homing instinct—that He placed inside many different species of birds.

I read recently about the Golden Plover. Native to Hawaii, the Plover migrates north during the summer to the Aleutian Islands. The Aleutian Islands are 1,200 miles away from Hawaii, and these little birds make the annual trek there, where they lay their eggs, and their little fledglings are born.

Then the adult Golden Plovers just leave, and the baby birds are left in the Aleutians to figure it out. Do you suppose the adults give the little ones some instructions?

No, they don't. There are no instructions, no maps, no globes, no laptops or iPhones with Mapquest, and no time schedules or calendars. The little birds are hatched, and without ever having been to Hawaii before, they just up and fly there on their own. How do they do that? God has placed a homing instinct inside of them. So the next time someone refers to you as a birdbrain, you can take it as a compliment.

I believe God has placed a homing instinct inside of us, too. It's an instinct—a desire—to go to a place where we have never been before. That place is called Heaven. The Bible says that God "has also set eternity in the human heart; yet no one can fathom what God has done from beginning to end" (Ecclesiastes 3:11, NIV). We long for this eternal place from the day we are born.

Even so, Heaven is *not* the default destination of every person. You don't get to go to Heaven because you are an American. It is only the destination of those who have put their faith in Jesus Christ as their Savior and Lord.

The Search

We start out our lives on a search. It begins in childhood. When we're just little children, we think to ourselves, *If I just got that toy I saw advertised on television, I know I would be happy.*

I remember one Christmas as a little boy when I got a pretty good haul of toys, and I was pretty happy about it. But then I went over to see what my friend had received for Christmas—and he had something that I wished I had. It was a little plastic scuba diver toy.

Understand that this was the 1960s, and toys were a little primitive then. You basically put two batteries in the little diver, dropped him into the water, and little bubbles came out of him.

Suddenly the stuff I had received didn't seem so good to me. I thought to myself, *I don't like anything that I have. I know I would be happy if I had that plastic scuba diver.* (It reminds me of the old saying "The only difference between men and boys is the price of their toys.")

And on and on it goes through life. You might say, "I would be happy if I had this sexual experience" or "I would be happy if I tried this drug" or "If I had this car . . . or boat . . . or motorcycle . . . or new home."

Do you know what all those longings really are?

They're a longing for God. Deep inside, that is what you are really looking for: God. You have a profound, innate desire for God printed on the very circuits of your soul.

And in the meantime your life speeds by. The older I get, the more I am amazed at how quickly times goes by. Toward the end of his life, King David prayed, "We are here for only a moment, visitors and strangers in the land as our ancestors were before us. Our days on earth are like a passing shadow, gone so soon without a trace" (1 Chronicles 29:15, NLT).

Before you know it, you're old. You always looked at "those old people," and then one day you look in the mirror, and you *are* one of those old people.

I heard about three guys who were buddies, and one day they discovered that they all shared the same birthday. On their fiftieth birthdays, they all decided they would go out and do something fun, and they were discussing where they might go.

One of the guys said, "I hear there's an amazing restaurant down by the water. They have really pretty waitresses. Let's go."

So they went to the restaurant and celebrated together. On their next decade birthday, at age sixty, they did it again.

One of them said, "Let's go back to that restaurant down by the water. They have really great food."

Then another ten years went by, and they were seventy. One of them said, "Let's celebrate down at that restaurant by the water again. They have great wheelchair ramps."

Then they hit eighty and were trying to figure out where they should go. Everyone was a little amazed that they were all still around.

One of them said, "I heard about a restaurant down by the water. Let's go there. We've never been there before."

That's the way it goes, isn't it? Before you know it, life has flown by, and then it's over. Then comes eternity. I think about people in my own life. Six years ago my son Christopher was here with us. Now he is in Heaven.

I still miss him deeply. Because it has been six years since his accident, people will say, "Are you over it?"

Don't ever ask someone who has lost a child if he or she is over it. You're never over it. You just get through it, day by day. I grieve to this day, but I do not grieve as one who has no hope. I grieve hopefully, because I know I will see him again. That's the hope of every Christian, the hope of Heaven.

A Christian never says good-bye to another Christian. We say, "See you later."

"See You in the Morning"

I heard the story of a Christian man who was terminally ill and on his deathbed. Knowing he had little time left, he called his three boys to his bedside—two of whom were believers. To his sons who had trusted Christ he said, "Good-bye boys, and I will see you in the morning."

Then he turned to his third son who wasn't a Christian. With sadness in his voice, the father said, "Good-bye, son."

The boy was distressed. "Dad, why did you say, 'See you in the morning' to my brothers but not to me?"

The father said, "Son, it's because you have never asked Jesus Christ into your life to be your Savior. What breaks my heart is that I will never see you again."

The boy began to weep and said, "But Dad, I *want* to see you again."

"Then you need to trust in Christ right now," he said.

And that's what the young man did. He prayed and accepted the Lord so that his father could say to him as well, "I will see you in the morning."

That is our hope.

Will I see you in the morning? Have you put your faith in Jesus?

Questions about Heaven

It's hard to wrap our minds around this place we have never been to. Part of our problem is that our minds have been filled with all sorts of caricatures of Heaven from Hollywood and cartoons and other sources. It's difficult for us to imagine what Heaven must really be like.

Is Heaven real? What will we do there? Will we know one another? What will our new bodies be like?

Let's think about some of those questions.

WHAT IS HEAVEN LIKE?

Heaven is an actual place. Just hours before His crucifixion, Jesus said to His men—and to all of us who know and love Him, "I go to prepare a place for you. And if I go and prepare a place for you, I will come again and receive you to Myself; that where I am, there you may be also" (John 14:2–3).

Heaven is a real place for real people to do real things. We often think of Heaven in a mystical way. Ridiculous pictures come to mind of people in floor-length robes, sitting on clouds, and plucking harps, with fat little baby angels hovering around. That is not a biblical Heaven; that is a cartoon Heaven. Heaven is a real place.

The Bible describes Heaven as a paradise. Again, remember that when Jesus died on the cross, a thief was crucified next to Him. Actually, he probably was more than a thief. He was most likely a murderer and an insurrectionist—someone today whom we might refer to as a terrorist. Looking over at the Lord, he said, "Jesus, remember me when you come into your kingdom" (Luke 23:42, NIV).

Jesus looked into the man's eyes and replied, "Truly I tell you, today you will be with me in paradise" (verse 43, NIV).

Heaven is a paradise.

The apostle Paul writes briefly about the experience of dying and going to Heaven. Yes, Paul was stoned. He was pummeled with rocks by his enemies and left for dead. During that interval, before he came back to life again, he entered Heaven itself.

Speaking about this experience, Paul wrote, "I know a man who, fourteen years ago, was seized by Christ and swept in ecstasy to the heights of heaven. I really don't know if this took place in the body or out of it; only God knows. I also know that this man was hijacked into paradise—again, whether in or out of the body, I don't know; God knows. There he heard the unspeakable spoken, but was forbidden to tell what he heard" (2 Corinthians 12:2–4, MSG).

"*This man was hijacked into paradise.*" What a picture.

Heaven is also a city. On more than one occasion the Bible describes Heaven with that term. Hebrews 11:10 speaks of Abraham "looking forward to the city with foundations, whose architect and builder is God" (NIV). In Hebrews 13, the writer says, "For here we do not have an enduring city, but we are looking for the city that is to come" (verse 14, NIV).

Think of any city you have been to in your life. What did you see there? Cities have roads, buildings, art, music, culture, goods, services, and events. So will Heaven. Don't think about sitting around on a cloud. Think of the best cities you have ever visited. Whatever greatness or beauty you have experienced on Earth will be so much better when you get to Heaven. Heaven is the original. Earth is the imitation.

The Bible describes Heaven as a country. In Hebrews 11:16, the writer speaks of God's people who "were longing for a better country—a heavenly one" (NIV).

Heaven is a country, a city, a garden, a paradise, a place.

Yes, in many ways, Earth is wonderful. We know that God created our world, and we celebrate His handiwork. Very honestly, I don't think anyone enjoys life on Earth more than a Christian. No one enjoys the beauty of a sunset more than a follower of Jesus Christ because we see the signature of our Father there. We know the God who did that. No one appreciates the love of family and friends more than a follower of Jesus Christ. The Bible says that "the earth is the Lord's, and all its fullness" (1 Corinthians 10:26).

When Jesus walked on our planet, He took time to admire a simple wildflower. Perhaps picking one up, He said, "Consider the lilies of the field, how they grow: they neither toil nor spin; and yet I say to you that even Solomon in all his glory was not arrayed like one of these" (Matthew 6:28–29).

Here is something we should all consider: For the Christian, living on this earth is as bad as it will ever get. But if you are a nonbeliever, this is as *good* as it's ever going to get.

We have a hope as Christians that as good as life is on this earth, better things are coming. The best is yet to come! That's extremely good news. God will give you a new body. No, you won't become another person; you still will be you. But you will be a radically upgraded version of you! The blueprints for your glorified body are in the body you now possess. Heaven is the earthly life of the believer, glorified and perfected.

On the other side, we will know more because we will be like Him. Sometimes people ask, "Will we know one another when we get to Heaven?"

Of course we will. Do you think you will be more stupid or insensible in Heaven than you are on Earth? We all will know so much more because God will give us that ability.

We will be reunited with friends and family. When Jesus died and rose from the dead, He appeared to His disciples. He was popping up practically everywhere. He was there with Mary at the tomb. He was there with the two disciples on the Emmaus Road. Then He was there with the fishermen apostles down by the Sea of Galilee. Then He appeared to five hundred people at once.

And with all of these people, it's as though He picked up right where He left off when He died. If you have a loved one in Heaven and belong to Christ yourself, you will see that loved one again.

What will we do in Heaven? We will worship the Lord, serve the Lord, and even eat in Heaven. It's true! The Bible says in Revelation, "Then the angel said to me, 'Write this: Blessed are those who are invited to the wedding supper of the Lamb!' " (19:9, NIV).

I love that word *supper*. I have a lot of friends in the South. When you're with them, and you're going out for dinner, they will sometimes say, "Let's have supper."

I was raised for a number of years by my grandparents. I called them Mama Stella and Daddy Charles. They were from Arkansas, and every night my grandmother would make a meal from scratch. We're talking here about the best fried chicken you have ever tasted. We're talking about black-eyed peas, mashed potatoes, collard greens, and amazing cornbread. But my grandmother's biscuits were the crowning achievement of her cooking. I've never had a biscuit like it before—or since. When those biscuits came out of the oven, they almost radiated with light. I feel almost certain that when we get to Heaven, the Lord will employ the abilities of my grandmother to make biscuits for us as we sit down and eat together.

Can you imagine not only being reunited with friends and family, but meeting the great patriarchs and matriarchs of the Scriptures? In Matthew 8:11 Jesus said, "And I say to you that many will come from east and west, and sit down with Abraham, Isaac, and Jacob in the kingdom of heaven."

Can you imagine sitting down and having a meal with these great men of God?

"*Moses, would you mind passing the manna?*"

"*Elijah, my meat is a little underdone. Could you give it a little more fire?*"

"*Lot, could you pass the salt? Oh Lot, you are so sensitive! Get over it.*"

Wait! There's More!

If there was only Heaven, it would be enough. As a Christian, however, you won't stay in Heaven forever. The Bible tells us that one day, Heaven will come to a new earth. This won't be a sequel; it will be a remake! God will remake all things:

> "And God will wipe away every tear from their eyes; there shall be no more death, nor sorrow, nor crying. There shall be no more pain, for the former things have passed away."
>
> Then He who sat on the throne said, "Behold, I make all things new."
> (Revelation 21:4–5)

That is what God will do. In this world to come, it will be out with the old and in with the new. As Chuck Swindoll writes in his excellent book on Revelation, "No more terminal diseases, hospitals, wheelchairs, or funerals. No more courts or prisons. No more divorces, breakdowns, or break-ups. No more heart attacks, strokes, Alzheimer's, or debilitating illnesses. No more therapists, medications, or surgery. No famines, plagues, or devastating disasters. *He is making all things new!"*[1]

We all like new stuff. A lot of people are excited about the next new iPhone. What will it be like? What will it do that the previous iPhone wouldn't do? People are intrigued by new technology, new outfits, new movies, and new cars.

God likes new stuff too—so much so that He will make *all* things new. Someday, if you are a Christian, you will have a new body living on a new earth. But all of that newness isn't just for the future. There is newness available right now.

He can make a new you *right now*. He can change you on the inside. The Bible says, "Therefore, if anyone is in Christ, the new creation has come: The old has gone, the new is here!" (2 Corinthians 5:17, NIV).

This is the hope of the believer. That is how we can have hope in this crazy world. My hope is not in politicians. My hope is not in government. My hope is not in manmade solutions. My hope is in God. He is the only One that keeps us going. There is a better world coming.

But all of these new and better hopes are for those who belong to Jesus Christ. I remember years ago when we used to wear Members Only jackets. What were we members of? I have no idea. But the beautiful scenes I have just painted of Heaven and the new earth are for *Christians only*.

What Will Happen to Those Who Aren't Christians?

I'm going to be straight with you. What happens to a non-Christian when he or she dies? The apostle John gives us the terrifying answer. Those who have never received Jesus Christ face a nightmare that never ends:

> Then I saw a great white throne and Him who sat on it, from whose face the earth and the heaven fled away. And there was found no place for them. And I saw the dead, small and great, standing before God, and books were opened. And another book was opened, which is the Book of Life. And the dead were judged according to their works, by the things which were written in the books. The sea gave up the dead who were in it, and Death and Hades delivered up the dead who were in them. And they were judged, each one according to his works. Then Death and Hades were cast into the lake of fire. This is the second death. And anyone not found written in the Book of Life was cast into the lake of fire.
> (Revelation 20:11–15)

This is an ominous scene. It is serious. It is sobering. And it may be the most tragic passage in the Bible. In

Dante's *Inferno*, the words written above the gates of Hell are "Abandon hope, all ye who enter here."

WHO WILL BE THERE ON THAT DAY?

Everyone who has rejected God's offer of forgiveness through Jesus Christ will be there on that day.

Adrian Rogers has a great outline in his book on Revelation, *Unveiling the End Times in Our Time*. I credit him with the following observations about who will stand before God's throne of judgment.[2]

Sinners will be there. Let me explain a little. There are a lot of sinners, and there are variations of sin. First, there will be the out-and-out sinners, as Dr. Rogers called them. These are people who hate God, have no belief at all, and go out of their way to mock Christians. They may be atheists or agnostics, and they scoff at the whole idea of God. They will find out the truth of that statement of Scripture that says, "Do not be deceived, God is not mocked; for whatever a man sows, that he will also reap" (Galatians 6:7).

Who else will be there?

Self-righteous people will be there. These people imagine that they are too good to face judgment. They may be kind and considerate. They may volunteer in their community. But they really don't think they need God. Being at this judgment will come as a shock to them. These are the people who believe they can earn their way to Heaven through good works. The Bible clearly says, however, that it is "not by works of righteousness which we have done, but according to His mercy He saved us" (Titus 3:5). Ephesians

2:8-9 ties a ribbon around that truth: "For it is by grace you have been saved, through faith—and this is not from yourselves, it is the gift of God—not by works, so that no one can boast" (NIV).

Who else will be there?

Procrastinators will be there. These are the people who may have been closer than the other two groups, but they were not close enough. These are people who weren't necessarily antagonistic toward the gospel. In fact, they would say things like, "I would like to believe in Jesus—and one of these days I think I will believe in Jesus." That day, however, never comes. And these people will experience God's judgment because they resisted God's offer and never made a decision.

Who else will be there? Church people will be there. By "church people" I mean those who went to church but didn't know God. Did you know that it's possible to go to church and not be a Christian? Going to a church doesn't make you a Christian any more than going to a doughnut shop makes you a police officer. (Sorry about that.) Going to church doesn't necessarily mean that you are a Christian. You can be baptized, receive communion, be accepted as a member of the church, and even walk down an aisle and say a little prayer. But if you never really put your faith in Christ, you could be there on this day. Why? Because you knew *about* God, but you didn't know God.

I think Jesus has a lot of followers like the so-called followers people have on Twitter: they're not really followers; they are observers.

Yes, church people will be there because they've led double lives, put on an act, and acted enough like a Christian to fool people. But their lives don't match their words. They talk about Heaven and live like Hell.

People like that aren't fooling God. You need to believe in Jesus and walk the walk as well as talk the talk.

For the people standing before God's Great White Throne of judgment, what they might have achieved on Earth won't matter in the least. It doesn't matter if they were kings and queens, presidents, emperors, rock stars, or billionaires.

The Bible says the books will be opened.

What is in these books?

One of them is probably a book of God's Law, or the commandments of God. The Bible says that God gave us the commandments "that every mouth may be stopped, and all the world may become guilty before God" (Romans 3:19). In other words, the Ten Commandments open our eyes (to our own lives) and shut our mouths (to any weak excuses).

Some people say, "I live by the Ten Commandments. That's all the religion I need."

I love it when people say that. I will reply, "Really? What are the Ten Commandments?"

"Uh . . ."

"Let me tell you a few of the Ten Commandments."

"Okay."

"You shall not take the Lord's name in vain. You shall not steal. You shall not lie. You shall not commit adultery.

Have you ever done any of those things?"

"No, never."

"And you are lying right now. Of course you've broken the commandments. We all have!"

The Bible says that if you have broken even one of the commandments, that is enough to keep you out of Heaven. The book of James says, "For whoever shall keep the whole law, and yet stumble in one point, he is guilty of all" (2:10).

Maybe another one of those books that will be open will be a record of every time one of those individuals heard the gospel of Jesus Christ.

Here on earth we have a record of so many things. At that time, there will be a record of every time you heard about Jesus dying for your sins. Perhaps there even will be a little replay of it.

There you are as a child in Sunday school.

There you are as a teenager walking down the street, and someone engages you in a conversation about Jesus Christ.

There you are at a church service.

There you are at a golf match, listening (impatiently) to someone speaking about their experience of knowing Jesus Christ.

There you are watching your television, listening to a preacher give the simple points of the gospel message at an evangelistic crusade in some stadium.

You will be held accountable for those exposures to the gospel. Why? Because knowledge brings responsibility.

Someone will usually say, "It's not fair. How could a God of love send people to Hell?"

Listen to me. This God of love doesn't *send* anyone to Hell. The last thing God wants to do is to see any man or woman uniquely made in His image end up in this place called Hell. The fact is that Hell was never made for people at all. Hell was made, according to Jesus, for the Devil and his angels (see Matthew 25:41). God wants you to go to Heaven. That is why He sent His Son on a rescue mission to this planet to be crucified on a Roman cross, to absorb God's wrath in our place, and to suffer and die and rise again so that you don't have to go to Hell.

In *The Great Divorce* C. S. Lewis wrote, " 'There are only two kinds of people in the end: those who say to God, "*Thy* will be done," and those to whom God says, in the end, "Thy will be done." All that are in Hell, choose it. Without that self-choice there would be no Hell.' "[3]

God doesn't want you to go there. He wants you to join Him in Heaven.

Choosing Your Eternal Address

Because God has given each one of us a free will, you can choose where you will spend eternity. You are the one who will decide your eternal address. You are the one who must choose whether you will go to Heaven—to that paradise, that better country, receiving a new body and being reunited with loved ones who have died in faith. Or, you can go to that place called Hell where you will be separated from God—and every hint of light, hope, or joy—for all eternity.

As the dying man told his sons, it's either "Good-bye" or "See you in the morning."

You don't go to Heaven to find Christ; you go to Christ to find Heaven. And you can do that right now.

"All right, Greg," someone may be saying. "I do want to go to Heaven. Tell me how."

Here's How

1. SIMPLY ADMIT THAT YOU ARE A SINNER

Yes, I know, that is hard for some people. But it's absolutely essential. Before you can be found, you have to admit to being lost.

In Romans 3:23 the Bible says, "For all have sinned and fall short of the glory of God."

Every one of us has broken God's commandments. Every one of us has fallen short of God's standards. I will certainly admit there are good people out there who are not Christians. To be really honest with you, I have met some non-Christians who are much nicer people than some Christians I have met. But being a good person doesn't get you to Heaven. *Heaven is not for good people; it is for forgiven people.* Even if you are a good person, relatively speaking, you aren't good enough.

You are not perfect, and Jesus said, "You shall be perfect, just as your Father in heaven is perfect" (Matthew 5:48).

But of course, on our own none of us are perfect, and none of us can become perfect. You fall short. You are a sinner. Recognize that and admit it to God.

2. REALIZE THAT JESUS CHRIST, THE SON OF GOD, DIED ON THE CROSS FOR YOUR SIN

Yes, He died for the world, but He also died for *you*. I love the way the apostle Paul personalizes it. He speaks of "the Son of God, who loved me and gave Himself for me" (Galatians 2:20).

Christ died for *you*. Truly. It wasn't nails that held Jesus to that cross more than two thousand years ago. It was love for you. As John 3:16 tells us, "For God so loved the world that He gave His only begotten Son, that whoever believes in Him should not perish but have everlasting life."

Let it sink in. Let it take root in your heart. Jesus Christ died for you.

3. YOU NEED TO REPENT OF YOUR SIN

What does that mean? It means realizing that you have done wrong things, that you keep doing wrong things, and that you are going to turn from these things and turn to Christ instead. The Bible says, "Repent, then, and turn to God, so that your sins may be wiped out, that times of refreshing may come from the Lord" (Acts 3:19, NIV).

4. YOU MUST RECEIVE JESUS CHRIST INTO YOUR LIFE

Being a Christian isn't merely believing a creed. It isn't merely going to a church. Being a Christian is having Jesus Christ live inside of you as Savior, as God, as Friend. Have you asked Him in yet? You will know if He is there. Jesus says, "Here I am! I stand at the door and knock. If anyone hears my voice and opens the door, I will come in" (Revelation 3:20, NIV).

Only you can do that. Only you can open the door of your life. No one else can open that door for you. The doorknob of your heart, so to speak, is on the inside. The Bible says, "But as many as received Him, to them He gave the right to become children of God, to those who believe in His name" (John 1:12).

If you have never done that, I'm going to ask you to do that right now. I'm going to ask you to do what almost 500,000 people have done over the past twenty-five years of our Harvest Crusades in stadiums in Southern California and around the world. I'm going to ask you to receive Christ, have your life changed, and have your eternal address changed.

5. YOU MUST DO IT PUBLICLY

When you have received Jesus into your life, I'm going to ask you, in some way, to make a public stand for Him, to tell people what you have done. Some two thousand years ago, Jesus died and bled for you publicly, and you need to own Him in your life without shame. Jesus said, "I tell you, whoever publicly acknowledges me before others, the Son of Man will also acknowledge before the angels of God" (Luke 12:8, NIV).

In our Harvest Crusades, I invite people in the stadium to walk down onto the field before the platform and make that public stand. The important thing is that you communicate before others that you have made Jesus Christ the Savior and Lord of your life. If you have the chance to do that in your church, take that opportunity. If you have a chance to tell your neighbors, your room-mates, your family, or people at your work that you have received Jesus, then take those opportunities. Doing so will not only please the Lord, but it will cement the deci-sion in your own heart and life.

6. DO IT NOW

If God has been speaking to your heart, you need to do this now—not tomorrow, not in a week, but *now*. This could be your last opportunity to get right with God because none of us knows when our lives will end.

You will never regret making this decision to follow Jesus. Not now. Not through all eternity.

Let's all pray together:

Father, I pray for those who are reading these words right now, whomever they are, wherever they are. You see them as individuals. You love them. You sent Jesus to die for them. I pray now that they will see their need for You and that they will come to You and receive the forgiveness that only You can offer. Lord, work mightily in these moments and bring this man or woman to Your-self. We ask all of this in Jesus' name. Amen.

.

NOTES

CHAPTER 1: GOD'S CURE FOR HEART TROUBLE

1. "Forty-two Percent of Americans 'Can't Live' without Cell Phone, Half Sleep with One," *ilookbothways.com*, http://ilookbothways.com/2009/11/02/42-of-americans-%e2%80%9ccan%e2%80%99t-live%e2%80%9d-without-cell-phone-half-sleep-with-one/.

2. Kathleen Fackelmann, "Stress Can Ravage the Body, Unless the Mind Says No," *USA Today*, March 21, 2005, http://usatoday30.usatoday.com/news/health/2005-03-21-stress_x.htm.

3. Lisa Miller, "Listening to Xanax," *New York*, March 18, 2012, http://nymag.com/news/features/xanax-2012-3/.

4. Jeffrey Kluger, "Fear Not! For Millions of Sufferers of Phobias, Science Is Offering New Treatments—and New Hope," *Time*, April 2, 2001, http://content.time.com/time/world/article/0,8599,2047666,00.html.

5. Alison Boshoff, "So Is Simon Cowell Cracking Up? 4 a.m. Phone Calls. 20-Hour Days. A 'Breakdown This Summer.' But That's Not the Half of It . . .," *The Daily Mail*, September 13, 2012, http://www.dailymail.co.uk/tvshowbiz/article-2203572/So-Simon-Cowell-cracking-4am-phone-calls-20-hour-days-A-breakdown-summer-But-thats-half-.html.

6. Phil Ferguson, "The Twelve Hottest Celebrity Atheists and Agnostics," *SkepticMoney.com*, January 17, 2012, http://www.skepticmoney.com/the-12-hottest-celebrity-atheists-and-agnostics/.

7. George Rush, Joanna Molloy, and Marcus Baram, "De Niro's Alibi 'Tale' Sought at Sex Trial," *New York Daily News*, April 2, 1998, http://www.nydailynews.com/archives/gossip/deniro-alibi-tale-sought-sex-trial-article-1.800544.

8. Holly McClure, "An Interview with Kevin Costner and Tom Shadyac," *Crosswalk.com*, http://www.crosswalk.com/print/1124986/.

9. Isaac Asimov, quoted in *Words from the Wise*, ed. Rosemary Jarski (New York: Skyhorse Publishing, 2007), 18.

10. C. S. Lewis, *The Complete C. S. Lewis Signature Classics* (New York: HarperCollins, 2002), 338.

11. C. S. Lewis, *The Business of Heaven: Daily Readings from C. S. Lewis* (New York: Houghton Mifflin Harcourt, 1984), 318.

12. Erik Hedegaard, "Still Crazy after All These Years," *Rolling Stone*, June 21, 2012, http://www.rollingstone.com/movies/news/still-crazy-after-all-these-years-20120621.

13. Brian Hiatt, "Paul McCartney: Yesterday and Today," *Rolling Stone*, June 18, 2012, http://www.rollingstone.com/music/news/paul-mccartney-yesterday-today-20120618.

CHAPTER 2: HOME BEFORE DARK

1. Lesley Savage, "Bradley Cooper Lives with His Mom, and He's Not Ashamed to Admit It," *CBS News*, April 17, 2013, http://www.cbsnews.com/news/bradley-cooper-lives-with-his-mom-and-hes-not-ashamed-to-admit-it/.

2. "Celebrity Atheist List," s. v. "William Shatner," *Celebathiests.com*, http://www.celebatheists.com/wiki/William_Shatner.

CHAPTER 4: GOD IN PURSUIT

1. Simon Vozick-Levinson, "Macklemore: Thrift Shop Hero," *Rolling Stone*, April 11, 2013, http://www.rollingstone.com/music/news/macklemore-thrift-shop-hero-20130411.

2. C. S. Lewis, *The Complete C. S. Lewis Signature Classics* (New York: HarperCollins, 2002), 604.

3. Josh Eells, "Gerard Butler's Wild Ride," *Men's Journal*, November 2012, http://www.mensjournal.com/magazine/gerard-butlers-wild-ride-20121126.

CHAPTER 5: HIGHWAY TO HEAVEN

1. Quoted in Jian Deleon, "Your Morning Shot: George Clooney," *GQ*, October 4, 2013, http://www.gq.com/style/blogs/the-gq-eye/2013/10/your-morning-shot-george-clooney.html.

2. Quoted in Randy Alcorn, *Heaven* (Wheaton, IL: Tyndale House Publishers, 2004), 33.

3. Ibid.

CHAPTER 6: HOW TO FIND ETERNAL LIFE

1. "Interviews," *Eminemworld.com*, http://www.eminemworld.com/interviews_freep_2000.php.

2. Tim Jonze, "Lana Del Rey: 'I Wish I Was Dead Already,' " *The Guardian*, June 12, 2014, http://www.theguardian.com/music/2014/jun/12/lana-del-rey-ultraviolence-album.

3. "Keith Urban Takes Broader View of Life," *Great American Country*, July 16, 2007, http://www.gactv.com/gac/cda/article_print/0,3008,GAC_26063_5631235_DS-ARTICLE-RIGHT-RAIL,00.html.

4. Associated Press, " 'I Am a Lonely Soul,' Boston Lead Singer Brad Delp Says in Suicide Note" *Fox News*, March 16, 2007, http://www.foxnews.com/story/2007/03/16/am -lonely-soul-boston-lead-singer-brad-delp-says-in -suicide-note/.

5. Brent Schlender and Steve Jobs, "The Three Faces of Steve: In This Exclusive, Personal Conversation, Apple's CEO Reflects on the Turnaround, and on How a Wunder-kind Became an Old Pro," *Fortune*, November 9, 1998, http://archive.fortune.com/magazines/fortune/fortune _archive/1998/11/09/250880/index.htm.

CHAPTER 7: SATISFACTION FOR THE SPIRITUALLY THIRSTY

1. Quoted in Richard Wagner, *C. S. Lewis and Narnia for Dummies* (Hoboken, NJ: Wiley Publishing, 2005), 318.

CHAPTER 8: THE PURSUIT OF HAPPINESS

1. Harry McCracken and Lev Grossman, "Google vs. Death," *Time*, September 30, 2013, http://time.com/574/google -vs-death/.

2. Steve Forbes, "Golden Times—Even If We Don't Know It," *Forbes*, April 27, 2007, http://www.forbes.com/ global/2007/0507/013.html.

3. Ann Oldenburg, "Chappelle Opens Up," *USA Today*, Feb-ruary 2, 2006, http://usatoday30.usatoday.com/life/ television/news/2006-02-02-chappelle_x.htm.

4. Rocco Parascandola, Vera Chinese, and Corky Siemaszko, "Exclusive: Co-hosts of Radio Show 'The Pursuit of

Happiness' Committed Suicide," *New York Daily News*, June 5, 2013, http://www.nydailynews.com/new-york/brooklyn/brooklyn-couple-committed-suicide-co-hosted-radio-show-article-1.1363804.

5. Gregg Easterbrook, "Money: The Real Truth about Money," *Time*, January 9, 2005, http://content.time.com/time/magazine/article/0,9171,1015883-1,00.html.

6. Quoted in Alister McGrath, *Intellectuals Don't Need God and Other Modern Myths* (Grand Rapids, MI: Zondervan, 1993), 15.

7. Wil S. Hylton, "What I've Learned: Hugh Hefner," *Esquire*, June 1, 2002, http://www.esquire.com/features/what-ive-learned/ESQ0602-JUN_WIL.

8. ABC News, "Johnny Depp Net Worth Still Sits on Top after Controversial Hollywood Film Awards Speech," *Foodworldnews.com*, November 16, 2014, http://www.foodworldnews.com/articles/8930/20141116/video-johnny-depp-net-worth-still-sits-on-top-after-controversial-hollywood-film-awards-speech.htm.

9. Brian Hiatt, "Johnny Depp: An Outlaw Looks at 50," *Rolling Stone*, June 18, 2013, http://www.rollingstone.com/music/news/johnny-depp-an-outlaw-looks-at-50-20130618.

CHAPTER 9: WHAT DO YOU LIVE FOR?

1. Donna Freydkin, " 'I Like My Odds' against Cancer, Michael Douglas Says," *USA Today*, September 11, 2010, http://usatoday30.usatoday.com/life/people/2010-09-10-1Adouglas10_CV_N.htm.

2.   Dave Itzkoff, "Woody Allen on Faith, Fortune Tellers and New York," *The New York Times*, September 14, 2010, http://www.nytimes.com/2010/09/15/movies/15woody.html?_r=0.

3.   Randy Alcorn, *Heaven*, xxi.

4.   Henry David Thoreau, *I to Myself: An Annotated Selection from the Journal of Henry D. Thoreau* (New Haven, CT: Yale University Press, 2007), 395.

5.   Rebecca Hardy, " 'I'm Quite Odd. I Do Get Very Dark Moods': Simon Cowell's Most Revealing—and Surprising—Interview Ever," *Mail Online*, http://www.dailymail.co.uk/tvshowbiz/article-1185451/Im-quite-odd-I-dark-moods-Simon-Cowells-revealing--surprising--interview-ever.html.

6.   Quoted in Carlos Wilton, *Lectionary Preaching Workbook, Series VIII, Cycle B* (Lima, OH: CSS Publishing Company, 2005), 214.

7.   Tammy Joyner, "More Businessmen Getting Cosmetic Surgery," Cox News Service, *Goupstate.com*, September 2, 2007, http://www.goupstate.com/article/20070902/NEWS/709020301.

CHAPTER 10: YOU MUST BE BORN AGAIN

1.   G. Campbell Morgan, *The Great Physician: The Method of Jesus with Individuals* (Eugene, OR: Wipf and Stock Publishers, 1937), 67.

2.   Dale Buss, "Christian Teens? Not Very," *The Wall Street Journal*, July 9, 2004, http://online.wsj.com/articles/SB108932505338159136.

3.   Ibid.

4. The Associated Press, "450 Sheep Jump to Their Deaths in Turkey," *USA Today*, July 8, 2005, http://usatoday30.usa-today.com/news/offbeat/2005-07-08-sheep-suicide_x.htm.

5. C. S. Lewis, *The Complete C. S. Lewis Signature Classics* (New York: HarperCollins, 2002), 50–51.

6. Max Lucado and Tricia Goyer, *3:16—The Numbers of Hope: A John 3:16 Book for Teens* (Nashville: Thomas Nelson, 2007), 6–7.

CHAPTER 11: TWO WORDS THAT CHANGED EVERYTHING

1. Austin Scaggs, "The Devil in Dave Matthews: Rolling Stone's 2004 Cover Story," *Rolling Stone*, June 23, 2011, http://www.rollingstone.com/music/news/the-devil-in-dave-matthews-rolling-stones-2004-cover-story-20110623.

2. Dave Matthews, vocal performance of "Trouble" by Kyle Brinson, Danny Harris, William Waring, Kurt Walker, and Stephen Rolfe Break, recorded September 23, 2003 with Dave Matthews Band on *Some Devil*, RCA, compact disc.

CHAPTER 12: FAMOUS LAST WORDS

1. *Famous Last Words: The Ultimate Collection of Finales and Farewells*, ed. Laura Ward (London: PRC Publishing Limited, 2004), 27.

2. *Famous Last Words*, 107.

3. Mary G. Boyer, *Arizona in Literature* (New York: Haskell House Publishers, 1934), 23.

4. Lynette Holloway, "Richard Versalle, 63, Met Tenor, Dies after Fall in a Performance," *The New York Times*, January 7, 1996, http://www.nytimes.com/1996/01/07/nyregion/richard-versalle-63-met-tenor-dies-after-fall-in-a-performance.html.

5. *Famous Last Words*, 82.

6. "Diana's Last Words Revealed for First Time in Report," December 17, 2006, *Mail Online*, http://www.dailymail.co.uk/news/article-423165/Dianas-words-revealed-time-report.html.

7. Quoted in Tim LaHaye, *The Merciful God of Prophecy: His Loving Plan for You in the End Times* (New York: Hachette Book Group, 2002), eBook edition.

8. Rochunga Pudaite and James C. Hefley, *The Greatest Book Ever Written* (Garland, TX: Hannibal Books, 1989), 54.

9. Bruce J. Evensen, *God's Man for the Gilded Age: D. L. Moody and the Rise of Modern Mass Evangelism* (New York: Oxford University Press, 2003), 3.

10. Quoted in *Tyndale Bible Dictionary*, eds. Walter A. Elwell and Philip Wesley Comfort (Carol Stream, IL: 2001), 421.

CHAPTER 13: HOW TO CHANGE YOUR LIFE

1. Edna Gundersen, "Madonna's Epiphany," *USA Today*, April 17, 2003, http://usatoday30.usatoday.com/life/2003-04-17-madonna-main_x.htm.

2. Ezra Klein and Evan Soltas, "Wonkbook: Eleven Facts about America's Prison Population," *The Washington Post*, August 13, 2013, http://www.washingtonpost.com/blogs/

wonkblog/wp/2013/08/13/wonkbook-11-facts-about
-americas-prison-population/.

CHAPTER 15: SEE YOU IN THE MORNING

1.   Charles R. Swindoll, *Insights on Revelation* (Grand
Rapids, MI: Zondervan, 2011), 274.

2.   Adrian Rogers and Steve Rogers, *Unveiling the End
Times in Our Time* (Nashville: B&H Publishing Group, 2013),
243–244.

3.   C. S. Lewis, *The Great Divorce* (New York: HarperCollins,
2001), 75.

GREG LAURIE

Greg Laurie is the senior pastor of Harvest Christian Fellowship in Riverside and Orange County in California. Harvest is one of the largest churches in the United States and consistently ranks among the most influential churches in the country. He recently celebrated forty years as the senior pastor. In 1990, he began holding large-scale public evangelistic events called Harvest Crusades. More than five million people have attended Harvest events around the world, and more than 421,800 people have registered professions of faith through these outreaches.

He is the featured speaker of the nationally syndicated radio program, *A New Beginning*, which is broadcast on more than seven hundred radio outlets worldwide. Along with his work at Harvest Ministries, he served as the 2013 honorary chairman of the National Day of Prayer and also serves on the board of directors of the Billy Graham Evangelistic Association.

He has authored over seventy books, including *As It Is in Heaven*; *Revelation: the Next Dimension*; *As I See It*; *Hope for Hurting Hearts*; *Married. Happily*; *Every Day with Jesus*; *Signs of the Times*; *Hope for America*; and many more.

He has been married to Cathe Laurie for forty years, and they have two sons, Christopher and Jonathan. Christopher went to be with the Lord in 2008. They also have five grandchildren.

For more information visit, www.allendavidbooks.com.